In the Presence of Buffalo

Working to Stop the
Yellowstone Slaughter

In the Presence of Buffalo

Working to Stop the Yellowstone Slaughter

Daniel Brister

WESTWINDS
PRESS®

THE PRUETT SERIES

First Edition 2013

Library of Congress Cataloging-in-Publication Data
Brister, Daniel.
    In the presence of buffalo : working to stop the Yellowstone slaughter /
Daniel Brister. — 1st ed.
      p. cm.
   ISBN 978-0-87108-978-6 (hardbound)
   ISBN 978-0-87108-959-5 (alk. paper)
   ISBN 978-0-87108-977-9 (e-book)
   1. American bison—Conservation—Yellowstone National Park. 2. Brucellosis
in cattles—Yellowstone National Park Region—Prevention—Government policy
Montana. I. Title.
   QL737.U53B746 2012
   599.64'3—dc23

                                  2012022533

WestWinds Press®
An imprint of Graphic Arts Books
P.O. Box 56118
Portland, OR 97238-6118
(503) 254-5591
www.graphicartsbooks.com

Cover design by Vicki Knapton
Book design by Kay Turnbaugh

This book is dedicated to my parents, Pindy and Bill, my brothers Billy and Charlie, my nephew Liam, and my wife, Andrea; to BFC cofounders Rosalie Little Thunder and Mike Mease; and to everyone who has ever volunteered to protect, taken action for, or been touched by wild buffalo.

Contents

Foreword

The Beast We Never Knew

REAT HERDS OF TOTEMIC ANIMALS HAVE THUNDERED THROUGH
human consciousness since the beginning of our kind. Today, we witness the tip of that ancient iceberg of animal craving when we witness the
wildebeests of the Serengeti or the caribou of the Arctic. But the greatest
herds ever to roam the face of the earth were the American bison of the
Great Plains. The numbers we hear stagger the imagination: 60 million
bison at the time of Lewis and Clark; a single herd of 10 million buffalo
taking several days to cross a great river in Iowa. Native Americans honored, preserved, and hunted this sacred beast for more than 13,000 years;
the birth of a white buffalo calf was a call to worship for Plains Indians. Yet
by 1902, the number of American bison remaining in the wild was twenty-
three animals.

The given reasons for their demise are the usual ones: Manifest Destiny, European dominion, the need for agricultural lands, or a way to deal
with the final solution to the Indian problem by eliminating the people's
commissary—the bison. We dealt with other Native inhabitants of North
America in much the same manner; the wolf and grizzly come to mind—
creatures that got in our way.

But there was something different about the way we went after the
buffalo. Unlike wily wolves or fierce grizzlies, the bison just stood there
and took it. Buffalo were killed for their hides and tongues, for sport, and
for the hell of it. The army gave out free ammunition to any dude riding the railroad who could shoot them from the train, leaving millions to
die and rot. Bison have a "ceremony of the dead," like elephants milling
around a fallen brother. Buffalo hunters could shoot a "stand" at great

distance, taking their time, killing as many as 120 bison from a herd in forty minutes.

It's impossible to imagine that magnitude of slaughter, killing that many huge mammals. How do we even think about one species inflicting near extinction on another large animal in a heartbeat of recent history? Between 1800 and 1893, white Europeans killed 50 million bison. Bull buffalo weigh up to a ton, cows less than half that. At an 800-pound average, 50 million buffalo would add up to 20 million tons of biomass. That's equal to all the sperm whales alive today; it's ten times the mass of all blue whales now swimming our oceans.

But none of this adds up to the real question: Why did the bison hold a place of such reverence and respect for Native Americans for millennia while European immigrants gleefully annihilated them in record time? Two cosmologies could not be more divergent. I've never quite been able to wrap my mind around this bedrock contradiction. Our American history books don't discuss this dark quandary that seems to represent the beginning of our Western relationship with the continent's wildlife and the land itself. To attempt to understand this particular breach of history is to beg the question of the nature of human attitudes toward the planet.

WestWinds Press® has published a new book by Dan Brister, *In the Presence of Buffalo: Working to Stop the Yellowstone Slaughter*. This is an important book in several respects.

For fifteen years, Dan Brister has followed the herds of Yellowstone's buffalo on the ground, on foot, across the snow-drifted sagebrush valleys, and into the lodgepole pine forests of our nation's oldest national park. Only a handful of modern people have peered so long and deeply into the eyes of wild American bison. He knows, as few do, the daily round, herd behavior, and seasons of the buffalo. Dan recognizes individual buffalo and senses the shaggy gravity in this huge dignified beast. He has come to love the solitary animals, herds, and the quintessential American species itself.

This is a particularly courageous time to publish a book on Yellowstone's buffalo. The senseless killing of bison continues today on public land, on the fringes of Yellowstone Park, this time led by the state of Montana's

Department of Livestock (DOL), aided and abetted by the National Park Service. Since the winter of 1996–97, the DOL and Park Service have shot and killed almost 4,000 wild, native bison. The pretense for the slaughter this time is a European cattle disease called brucellosis. Cows gave it to elk and buffalo; there is no documentation of bison ever giving it back to cattle in the wild. The only wild, free-ranging herd of American bison on earth is no longer allowed to roam free.

Dan Brister's book bears witness to the last fifteen years of this bureaucratic madness to tame the last vestige of wild America and domesticate the earth. Leading the resistance is the Buffalo Field Campaign, a brave, dedicated group of activists. This hardy tribe lives out in the cold winters of Yellowstone, risking their freedom and lives to stand by their brown brethren in the hair coats.

I have a great deal of respect for the buffalo warriors; their very presence at the dying fields where Yellowstone's buffalo are shot down by DOL agents brings us again to the lingering question of what kind of mindless hate could have allowed us to kill 60 million buffalo in a single century. Is it a kind of original sin, a hopeful vision of the frontier replaced with a cast of butchers? Defending the right of the buffalo to return may allow us to readdress an ancient historical insult.

My own partisan views are carved from decades of watching buffalo. Forty years ago, I lived alone in the backcountry of Yellowstone for months at a time filming grizzly bears. Back in the 1970s, grizzlies were less common; sometime you didn't see a bear for a week or more. But the buffalo were there, every day, prancing and rolling and bellowing—dominating the landscape. Watching them became an entire way of thinking. And these bison were the great, great, many times great grandchildren of those twenty-three buffalo they couldn't catch in Yellowstone's Pelican Valley in 1902. Their kinship gave me immense pleasure. May our own grandchildren someday share this vision of America's quintessential animal?

—Doug Peacock

Introduction

Buffalo or Bison

LIKE SO MUCH ELSE ABOUT AMERICAN BUFFALO, WHAT WE CALL THEM can be a source of great contention. While bison, or more specifically *Bison bison bison*, is the species' scientific name, I usually call them buffalo. I have had people take great offense to my use of this word, telling me I should know better and accusing me of conveying false information.

According to the *American Heritage Dictionary*, both words are correct. Buffalo, from the French *beoufs*, and bison, from the Greek, mean roughly the same thing: oxlike creature. In reference to the North American species, buffalo has been used longer and is more deeply ingrained in the American consciousness while bison, from a purely taxonomical standpoint, is more accurate. But despite the fact that the species is more closely related to the European wisent than to the buffalo of Asia and Africa, I still stick with buffalo.

I prefer the sound of the word and its more familiar common usage in the American vernacular. I like the memories and dreams it stirs, and its power to bring to life, if nowhere else but our imagination, the days when millions roamed our prairies. I like the way the word rumbles from deep in the chest and rises from within, migrating through the body with a resonance like the bass beat of hooves on hard earth.

one

Breaking Trail

I HAVE A BAG OF BUFFALO HAIR, GATHERED FROM THE BARK OF TREES during recent springs. When I collect enough I'll have it spun. Next winter I will wear a buffalo-wool hat on patrol. It will make me more effective—more familiar to the shaggy giants as I stand with them on the national forestlands where they have been killed by the thousands in recent years. Maybe they'll catch the scent of their kin in my cap and know I am different from the ones with guns who plague their winter days.

My relationship with the buffalo is in its fifteenth year. We have spent many a cold and quiet sunrise together. The first winter I was with them nearly every day, standing watch for the livestock agents on their noisy snowmobiles. Most days the agents never came, leaving us to the peace and beauty of the Yellowstone area, free to observe the buffalo on their terms, browsing on their native habitat.

With the passing of time, I find myself in their presence less often, working instead with their images in word, video, and photograph to convey to the world a sense of what is happening to this last wild herd. I know this is a trade-off, that my work in the office is crucial, yet at times I need to renew the bonds, to leave the computers and ski out to the boundary and spend a morning patrol with the buffalo.

Human beings and bison—or buffalo as they have come to be called—have a rich relationship going back at least 300 centuries. One of the oldest known works of art in the world, a painting on the wall of Chauvet Cave beside the Ardéche River in France, depicts bison in vivid detail and is believed to be 32,000 years old. In North America, heaps of bones, stone points, and butchering tools have been excavated from the bases of cliffs throughout the northern plains. These artifacts, and the landscapes in which they are found, tell the story of the continent's longest-running human–animal relationship. One of the more famous of these buffalo jumps, Head Smashed In, is located in southern Alberta, Canada. Because of its nearly perfect geography, virtually every cultural group to inhabit the area during the last 8,000 years hunted bison at Head Smashed In.

When most people think of Native American buffalo hunts, they picture horse-mounted Indians pursuing bison on horseback, hunting with spears or arrows. Yet this image, so strong in the popular consciousness, is misleading. The stereotypical image of the horse-mounted hunter that we have come to identify with the Great Plains tribes existed for less than two centuries. Before Europeans introduced the horse, indigenous North Americans hunted buffalo on foot, praying, luring, coaxing, and chasing them off cliffs at such sites as Head Smashed In, the Madison River, Chugwater, and Bonfire Shelter.

The Blackfeet people, who occupy the heart of buffalo-jump country, use the word *piskun* to refer to the jumps, meaning "deep blood kettle" and a fitting description of what a recently used jump must have looked like. Located in what is today known as southern Alberta, Head Smashed In earned its name over thousands of years. This site resembles other jumps in its geology and geography.

Hunters would wait for a large herd to gather on a rolling plateau above a small cliff. Others would hide downwind while a buffalo caller, prepared for his work through days of fasting and prayer, drew the attention of the buffalo and started them moving in the general direction of the cliffs. Once the animals were moving, people would emerge from hiding and herd the buffalo from behind, chasing them into the mouths of funnel-shaped drive lanes. The lanes were marked by hundreds of stone cairns or "dead men" that were sometimes piled with brush or hides. As the herd stampeded through the narrowing lanes, people popped up from behind these cairns to dissuade the frightened animals from veering off and escaping. The lanes always led to a cliff, which, from above, looked like only a gentle change in grade. The lead buffalo, realizing only at the last moment what lay ahead, had no choice but death, pressed from behind by the momentum of the herd. Over the cliffs they spilled by the hundreds. The cacophony of crashing tons of flesh and snapping bone must have shaken the earth and stirred the hearts of all who heard it. Men with stone-tipped spears stood poised near the bottom, killing those not lucky enough to die from the initial plunge.

The real work began after the buffalo were killed. Hunting on the jumps was a community undertaking involving hundreds of people. Butchering so many buffalo was a monumental task. Because the meat would spoil quickly, it had to be cut from the carcass and sliced into thin strips for drying as fast as possible. Buffalo were skinned and butchered with stone tools, and the meat was sun dried or smoked to preserve it for the coming winter. Failure in any aspect of the jump's orchestration could mean a very difficult winter with widespread starvation and sickness.

The sheer numbers of buffalo on the plains—estimates range from twenty to sixty million at the time of European contact—together with the communal technology of the jump, provided the foundation for the longest sustained lifestyle in North American history. The jump was a popular means of hunting buffalo from prehistoric times all the way to the mid-1800s. The last known use of a jump took place around 1850, by which time Indian and white hunters with guns, wastefully killing to supply an insatiable market for buffalo hides in the eastern United States, had so depleted the herds that the use of the jump became impractical.

The mass eradication of wild bison from the plains forever altered the balance of life in North America. By the end of the nineteenth century, with wild buffalo all but gone, virtually every Native American tribe had been eradicated or forced into a sedentary lifestyle on a reservation. The fate of the buffalo was much the same. When the great herds were decimated in the West, a few individuals holed up in Yellowstone's Pelican Valley, one of the country's coldest and most snowy valleys, and avoided extinction.

In 1902, twenty-three free-ranging bison were all that remained in the United States. Fearful that such a small herd would suffer from inbreeding, park managers procured at least fourteen captive buffalo from a ranch in

Montana's Flathead Valley and three from the Texas Panhandle. The existence of these private herds, both of which were established at the peak of bison decimation in the 1870s, resulted from the efforts of a few individuals. Samuel Walking Coyote, a Pend d'Oreille Indian from northwestern Montana, and Mary and Charles Goodnight, a Texas ranching couple, helped ensure the survival of the species.

In the early 1870s, Walking Coyote left his native Flathead Valley and traveled east, crossing the Continental Divide to hunt buffalo on the Rocky Mountain Front in northern Montana and southern Alberta. Due to the growing scarcity of bison, his hunts were largely unsuccessful. On one scouting trip, Walking Coyote's party encountered a group of orphaned calves. The young bison, lonely for their mothers, took to Walking Coyote's horses. Thinking they would make a good gift to his people, he returned to the Flathead Valley with six calves in the spring of 1873. A decade later, when he sold them to neighboring ranchers Michel Pablo and Charles Allard, Walking Coyote's herd had increased to thirteen animals. By 1895, the Pablo–Allard herd was 300 strong.

At about the same time as Walking Coyote's hunting trip, Mary Goodnight was witnessing the rapid disappearance of the buffalo on the Texas panhandle grasslands surrounding the ranch she shared with her husband. She persuaded him to capture a small group of bison and bring them onto the ranch, where they'd be safe from the hunters. Goodnight ranch hands roped and captured two bison calves. Over the next decades, through additional capture and breeding, the herd increased steadily. By 1910 the Goodnights had 125 bison on their ranch.

Twenty-one buffalo from these two private herds were introduced to Yellowstone's Lamar Valley in 1902. Over time, members of the Lamar herd mingled with members of Yellowstone's indigenous Pelican Valley herd. Although the extent of interbreeding is not known, their progeny are the roughly 4,000 Yellowstone buffalo living today. They are both behaviorally and genetically unique. Members of the only herd in America not confined by a fence, they carry a direct genetic link to Yellowstone's original population, a subspecies of the large, curly haired bison known as wood or mountain bison (*Bison bison athabascae*). The Yellowstone herd is believed to carry genes from both the wood and the more common plains subspecies (*Bison bison bison*).

During the winter of 1996–97, more buffalo were killed than in any single year since the 1870s. In the early months of 1997, the Montana Department of Livestock (DOL), with cooperation from the National Park Service, killed 1,084 Yellowstone buffalo. Starvation was common that winter, when early January rains blanketed the ground with a thick slab of ice. Record levels of snow and cold followed. Buffalo, braced against blizzard, nuzzled tons of snow aside only to scrape their noses on diamond-plated ice. Between the human slaughter and the natural deaths, over 2,000 animals—more than half the population—were destroyed in a matter of months.

I moved to Missoula that wicked winter, barely aware of what was happening a few hundred miles away. The slaughter was one of those distant news stories that made me cringe but didn't seem to bear on my immediate life. The headlines caught my attention, but I didn't know how to help. I was in my room on Fifth Street, studying the peeling paint on the windowsill, when I heard on public radio that the kill tally outside Yellowstone had surpassed a thousand. A thousand: I didn't even know that there were a thousand wild buffalo left.

When I learned that they were being slaughtered in and around Yellowstone, I knew I had to act. Yellowstone had changed my life, giving me the courage and drive to move away from the East, from what was familiar. Yellowstone confirmed my suspicion that I was happier in the mountain wilds of the West than on the crowded shores of Cape Cod that had shaped the first eighteen years of my life and the lives of my ancestors since the seventeenth century.

The son of a Cape Cod fisherman, I didn't have the option, or the inclination, to follow in my father's boots. He was among the last generation of fishermen to reap the harvest of cod from the once-abundant waters of the north Atlantic. When John Cabot, in 1497, encountered the grounds on which my father would later fish, he said that they were so "swarming with fish [that they] could be taken not only with a net but in baskets let down with a stone." Like many of the places in the West named after an abundance of species that have since departed—Salmon, Idaho, and Buffalo, Wyoming, come immediately to mind—my native landscape is drifting farther and farther from its namesake. I remember my father's worry over the ever-increasing presence of factory trawlers and draggers that were so efficient at depleting the fish stocks and destroying their ocean-bottom habitat. Like the nineteenth-century buffalo hunters, my father and his fellow fishermen didn't believe that they were guilty of pushing the cod toward oblivion. But the armada of small boats like my father's *Madonna* plying the waters off of the Eastern Seaboard must have taken a toll. After the crash, the government began buying boats from the small fishermen, severely limiting the number of licenses and amount of time a boat could spend at sea. But these measures were much too little way too late; codfish are following fast on the heels of the buffalo.

I traveled west the summer before my senior year of college at the University of Vermont. I spent three months backpacking in the Rockies, exploring the mountains of Colorado and Wyoming, and walking the beaches of northern California. In early September, on my way back to Vermont and not wanting my time in the West to end, I stopped in Yellowstone for one final immersion in the woods.

There I found what I'd never even known I'd lost. Never having been in Yellowstone, I relied on the recommendations of a backcountry ranger to plan the excursion. She directed me to a loop through a series of lakes. When I hit the trail, I was shocked to discover a blackened world. I hiked for miles through the burnt terrain, my mouth dry, black streaks on my legs, face, and hands from brushing against charred trees. The silence was broken only by the dry and incessant clack of some kind of insect. Everything was black, white, or gray. When I reached the designated campsite, where a wooden sign was tacked onto a burnt pole and carved with "G3," I was feeling a bit down. This wasn't why I had come to Yellowstone. Images of destruction, of bombed-out cities, cluttered my consciousness.

The next day I noticed the new growth. Trees three feet tall and seeming to glow green from within were scattered everywhere. I hadn't even seen them the day before. Overwhelmed by the fire's power to destroy, I had missed its creative potential, the future forest that had established itself in the four years since the great fire. I began to let go of my craving for the life-brimmed landscapes I had expected of Yellowstone, accepting the fire's power and the resilience of the new generation of trees. At day's end, I walked around a bend in the trail into a clearing. Before me lay Wolf Lake, rimmed by a grove of green trees and lush grass. As I walked into the meadow, the most amazing bird of my life—I have since learned it was a giant sandhill crane—rose from the grass in a widening spiral and vibrated my breastbone with a deep and primal liquid call. My eyes, rising with the crane, were arrested in the gaze of an elk across the meadow. I can't say how long we stood staring into each other, but it might have been forever had the elk not turned away and vanished.

After making camp, I cooked a dinner of rice and beans. Marveling at the alchemical ability of the backcountry to transform bland food into a gourmet treat, I ate on the lakeshore, absorbing sunset. I wasn't sitting long when, from the woods across the lake, a bull moose and two calves came sauntering toward the water. I watched as they faced off in a triangle and pawed at the lake, repeatedly kerplunking their hooves in the water. The bull galloped through the shoals, dropped his head to dunk an antler, and shot sparks of liquid silver into the air above the lake and the faces of the calves. The moose trio cavorted in the shoals for more than an hour before leaving the lake in silence and blending back into the trees. I sat alone on the far shore in the fading day, baptized by the splash of moose.

Before my trip out West, I had never been in the woods with moose, elk, or bison. I'd never spent time in grizzly bear country or, sharks excepted, felt the presence of predators. Although I'd camped in the Northeast, this had been meager preparation for the magnitude of wild in the West. Never before had I felt the humming of my every cell, my senses so open to the world around me. This was living.

Wrapped that night in the cocoon of my sleeping bag, I stared into the stars, awestruck at the twisting of the sky around Polaris. In and out of sleep I drifted, noting the rising and falling of individual stars and creating constellations of my own. I had never taken the time to engage in such intimacy with the night. While I knew that the North Star never moved, I had failed to consider the journeys of the other stars and the overall pattern of the spinning sky. I stayed up most of the night reveling in my new discoveries.

After sunrise, I fell deeply asleep. That's when she came to me. My mother, dead five years, looked straight into my eyes. Her face was illuminated against a darkness as deep and clear as the one that had framed the stars. We spoke, face to face, for hours. When I woke, sweating in the downstuffed sack, the sun was already high in the sky. I tried to grasp the words she'd come to speak, but they leaked through my mind like sand sifting through a child's fingers at the beach. Her face had been a few feet from my own, and we'd been discussing the direction of my life like a mother and her twenty-two-year-old son might do over coffee. Her features were her own healthy ones, and her head was capped with her trademark dark brown curls that had earned her the nickname "Poodle" from her brothers. Never much of a fan of those particular dogs, I'd always wished they'd come up with a different name for her, something that better captured her independence and strength. If her brothers had been familiar with the shaggy giants, perhaps they would have named her "Buffalo" after the wood bison's dark and curly wool.

I have a picture of my mother cracking meat from a lobster's claw. It is the happiest image I have of her. She's looking into the camera, her whole face glowing with a smile. As I type these words, I am looking at this photo and thinking back to the clambakes we used to have on the shore of Cape Cod Bay. My mother, of all her brothers and sisters, was most intimate with the traditions of old Cape Cod. They all spent their childhood summers there, but my mother was the first to take the plunge and stay year-round. This, combined with the fact that she had married a local fisherman whose ancestors had called the peninsula home for three and a half centuries, marked my mother as a true Cape Codder in the eyes of her siblings. I can see this in the way she presides over the table, in the way she cracks the lobster's claw, and in the confidence behind her smile. I look to this photo when I need to be reminded of my true mother and escape the torment of later memories of her sickness.

Bald from the chemotherapy that plagued the final years of her life, the image I remember most clearly before she died is her bloated face, contorted in pain. I shared her sadness and frustration as she stood before her bedroom mirror in the ill-fitting wig, a parody of her natural curls. I remember lying awake in my room at the far end of the hall, staring at too-familiar configurations of cracks on my moonlit bedroom wall as she limp-paced up and down the hallway, pleading to her foot cramps, "Please, please, please, go away!" A recurrent nightmare from which neither of us could wake.

But that September morning in Yellowstone my healthy mother came to see me—the woman who would goof off to songs on the car radio, making up her own silly words and coaxing me to join her. She'd sing and laugh, trying to make me smile with her funny faces. My teenage self, too cool for goofing off, was embarrassed by my dork of a mother.

She was neither playful nor sad in the Yellowstone dream. Much of our conversation fell away from my waking mind as my eyes opened beside Wolf Lake. But the few grains of her parting words remained. "The path you are on is right," she said. "I am with you." Her words gave me the confidence to make difficult choices. Although I already knew—on some level—that I needed to be an activist and to align my life with my beliefs, I was full of doubt. How would I support myself? What would my family think? Would I be able to find work that fit my skills and beliefs? I had been battling with this internal conflict all summer, and my mother's reassuring words removed my doubt. Kneeling in the grass by the lake, I let go of my fear and began to follow my heart.

—·—

Five years later I sat in my Missoula room in the wake of a news report on the slaughter of more than a thousand Yellowstone buffalo. That afternoon, I started doing research and educating myself, trying to uncover the reason, if there was one, for the slaughter. I struggled to find sense in the actions of the Montana government. Buffalo were being killed at the insistence of the livestock industry because some of them carried a European disease—brucellosis—that they originally contracted from cattle. Despite the fact that there was not a single documented case of wild bison transmitting the disease to livestock, buffalo leaving the park and entering Montana were being slaughtered to protect a few hundred Idaho cattle. Because the cattle are only in the area between June and October, a time when the bison are deep within the park, there is no way in which they could transmit the disease. Elk also carry brucellosis but, unlike bison, don't raise the ire of the livestock industry.

The following winter I learned of a group of people running daily patrols from a rented cabin, intent on stopping the slaughter. Armed with video cameras and direct-action tactics, Buffalo Field Campaign volunteers were spending all of their days with the bison, monitoring migrations out of the park and interfering with the DOL's slaughter operations. As soon as I could, I traveled to West Yellowstone to help them. Originally planning on a weeklong visit, before the week was up I'd revised my plans to spend the winter. Since that week in December 1997, I have worked with the campaign as a volunteer, a media coordinator, a member of the group's board of directors, and currently, an executive director. In the intervening years, more than 4,000 volunteers from around the world have joined us. From them I have learned a powerful lesson: Apathy is not omnipotent.

One of the more challenging periods of our early years came in February and March 1999, when more than eighty buffalo, following Duck Creek out of the park, stood poised on the boundary, sniffing hay that had been put out to lure them into a capture facility set up on private land adjacent to Yellowstone. Knowing the animals would be slaughtered if they followed their instincts to the hay, we determined to make a human shield between the hungry bison and the food they needed so badly. Dissuading a 2,000-pound bull from fresh hay is no easy task. Attempting to hold back twenty hungry bulls, fifty cows, and ten calves is futile.

For more than a month we maintained around-the-clock patrols at Duck Creek, weighing the evil of starvation against the certain death of the cage. A debate arose among the activists, some feeling that our incessant presence on the boundary was too intrusive and would erode the animals' wildness, while others argued that the alternative—capture and slaughter—

was far worse. This ideological divide between volunteers rears its head each winter and, depending on the situation, is usually resolved during nightly meetings, when the next day's strategy is planned. In this case, consensus was reached without much fuss. The baited bison trap was a strong deterrent to letting the buffalo pass.

The midnight-to-sunrise shift at Duck Creek is savored by volunteers who enjoy hunkering through the night before the flicker of a small fire, taking warming ski trips to check on bedded bison, and watching as droplets of dawn wash darkness away. Sunrise is reason enough for me to brave the cold nights, although beauty on the western boundary is always tainted with the ever-present fear of capture and slaughter.

Early on the morning of March 14, five very determined bulls pushed by us. Within minutes, the DOL had them in their trap, the heavy steel doors locked behind them. A few days later, three bulls took a path that we had shoveled through the snow for them, a detour around the trap. Over the next few days, the pressure began to ease as more and more of the herd followed the new route.

Whenever buffalo traveled this path, a crew of volunteers followed at a respectful distance to ensure that the animals weren't hit as they crossed the highway or chased by DOL agents back to the trap. On a March afternoon in 1999, I followed four very large bull bison down this well-trodden trail accompanied by my good friend Pete. A farmer from Driggs, Idaho, Pete has been volunteering with the campaign since its inception in 1997. Because buffalo are out of the park in the winter months when Idaho crops won't grow, Pete's farm life allows him to devote his winters to the buffalo.

As we neared U.S. Highway 191, a north-south corridor paralleling the park's western boundary, we coordinated the road crossing. With a two-way FM radio, I let our friends on the highway know that we were coming. By the time the bulls reached the roadside, Jessie and Mike were in place, Jessie fifty yards to the south and Mike fifty yards to the north. Both held large "Bison Crossing" signs to advise passing motorists. Chipmunk warned approaching semis over the CB from the front seat of the campaign truck. A woman driving a Subaru with Alberta plates wisely stopped her car, then stared as the four bulls, each weighing nearly a ton, crossed less than three feet from her front bumper.

Once they were across the highway, the bulls chose the Cougar Creek snowmobile trail to carry them across seven miles of national forest to the far side of Horse Butte. A peninsula teeming with wildlife—including threatened and endangered species like grizzly bears, wolves, bald eagles, and trumpeter swans—Horse Butte is the favored winter habitat of the Yellowstone bison. Due to the butte's wide expanses of sun-drenched, south-facing slopes, the snow melts fast, providing easy access to last summer's grass in the winter and the first green shoots in the spring.

Pete and I followed the bulls toward Horse Butte, relieved that the bottleneck by the trap had finally been broken. We made up funny songs about buffalo and sang others that our friends had written. On our way to the butte, we talked about a day when the buffalo would be treated like deer and elk, allowed to move freely between Yellowstone and the surrounding lands. "You hear that?" Pete shouted to the bulls. "You're going to be free, just like you used to be!" Although we didn't know it at the time, Pete and I would spend the coming night in jail.

With the December 2000 signing of a new bison-management plan, which is set to be in effect until 2015, freedom for the buffalo seems far away. The new plan, agreed upon and signed by the heads of federal and state agencies, calls for the continued slaughter of buffalo on public lands surrounding Yellowstone, sets a politically derived population cap on the herd, and imposes a management regimen of heavy-handed human interference.

Since my first ski patrol along the Yellowstone boundary, the DOL and Park Service have killed more than 3,800 buffalo. During the single winter of 2007–8, the worst single year for the species since the nineteenth century, more than 1,600 buffalo were slaughtered or shot, most without being tested for brucellosis. Hopeful in the early days for a quick end to the killing, we've had to adjust our plans to reflect the reality that our presence in the field will likely be needed for years to come. Today's Yellowstone herd faces a situation similar to that of its ancestors of a hundred years ago. If history continues on its present course, the Yellowstone herd will become just another intensively managed, domesticated herd, and the thin thread so tenuously linking our present century to the wild and fertile past will be forever severed.

In 1970, a few months after I was born, National Park Service research biologist Mary Meagher remarked, "The present bison population is completely wild and unfettered by fencing and artificial management." Reading this today saddens me, for the statement no longer holds true. Although the Yellowstone buffalo remain unfenced, they are hardly unfettered. Each winter when they leave the park in search of grass, they fall victim to intense artificial management.

Until they are once more wild and unfettered, I will continue to work for their protection. On patrol, I pluck bison hair from the bark of trees. It has become a means of measure for me, a way to weigh my time in the field. One of these winters I will wear a buffalo-wool hat.

Negligent Endangerment

A FEW HOURS AFTER CROSSING THE HIGHWAY WITH PETE AND the four bulls on that March afternoon in 1999, I found myself locked in a cell with a guy who thought that the Grizzly Discovery Center was Yellowstone National Park. "I've always heard about all the bears and wild animals in Yellowstone," he told me. "But there are only four bears and a few wolves in cages." I tried to let my cell mate know that he was mistaking a makeshift zoo for the world's oldest national park, but never having been out of Florida, he couldn't be convinced.

Locked in our concrete room, we explained our arrests to one another. I sat on the cold steel cot with the back of my head resting against the wall while he stood at the door squeezing the bars with white-knuckled hands. Michael was a wiry man, about five foot eight. His hair was nearly the same shade of brown as mine, almost black. A tentacled blotch of green marred the cheek below his left eye. After puzzling over the design for a while, I realized it was a tattoo of a marijuana leaf.

"Me and the old lady," he said, turning to face me, "are on an epic road trip. We left St. Petersburg on New Year's with fifty-three bucks between us. It's so easy," he said. Then he told me how they'd been financing their travels: "Just find a bank that lets you open a checking account with no minimum balance. They'll give you a whole book of checks for twenty bucks."

The first account took them through New Orleans for Mardi Gras and then west to Salt Lake City. He explained how convenient highway-side convenience stores can be. "Once you pump your gas, they have no choice but to take your check. But most places don't even run them." In Salt Lake City, they stopped for a rest and exchanged a friend's address and twenty bucks for a new account and a new book of checks. Their trail of insufficient funds finally caught up with them in West Yellowstone, where an Econo Mart clerk called the sheriff per the urgings of her instant-verification machine. The officer who pulled them over, Michael told me, "found some meth in the casing of our interior light."

He had as much trouble understanding my arrest as I did his misconceptions about Yellowstone. His face scrunched into a bewildered grimace as I explained how I had ended up in jail. He couldn't wrap his mind around the idea of me and my four friends—who were being held in separate cells—risking our freedom to protect buffalo from the DOL.

"Why the hell would you go to jail over buffalo?" he wanted to know.

Like most people, my cell mate that night was unaware that a herd of continuously wild, free-ranging buffalo had survived the nineteenth-century slaughter by taking refuge in the remote backcountry of Yellowstone's Pelican Valley. Yellowstone National Park is the only place in America where wild bison were not eradicated. By 1902, the innumerable herds, which once occupied much of North America and numbered in the tens of millions, had been reduced to a single herd of less than two dozen individuals.

The miraculous recovery of the Yellowstone population is widely viewed as America's most successful conservation achievement. Yet it is a tenuous achievement at best. Yellowstone buffalo are being killed in greater numbers today than at any time in the last hundred years.

To the westward-expanding Euro-Americans, bison slaughter was synonymous with settling the West. The men who cleared away the buffalo were proud of their achievement. History books hold photos of massive skull and bone mountains with men poised triumphantly on their summits. They relate stories of bison being gunned down for their hides and tongues—an East Coast delicacy—or for "sport" from moving trains, the carcasses left to rot on the prairies. Americans took pride in the eradication of the buffalo, identifying the slaughter as a distinctly American pastime. Theodore Davis, writing for *Harper's* in January 1869, invoked patriotism to describe the wasteful slaughter:

It would seem to be hardly possible to imagine a more novel sight than a small band of buffalo loping along within a few hundred feet of a railroad train in rapid motion, while the passengers are engaged in shooting, from every available window, with rifles, carbines, and revolvers. An American scene, certainly.

Americans like Tom Nixon, who bragged of cutting down 120 buffalo in forty minutes in 1876, were well known and admired in their day, and history has immortalized such killers as "Buffalo" Bill Cody, who is said to have taken the lives of 4,280 buffalo in eighteen months.

More than 130 years later, the age of eradication continues. Although the brush with extinction roused strong public sentiment against the men who brought it on, some still attempt to emulate the exploits of the great killers. Tom Nixon and Buffalo Bill have their twenty-first-century counterparts.

"I've shot more than a thousand head," an agent named Dave bragged when I met him on the bluffs above the Madison River in March 1998. Dave is a modern-day buffalo hunter whose love for his line of work has resulted in an interesting employment history. Working as a game warden for the Montana Department of Fish, Wildlife, and Parks (FWP) in the early 1990s, he and the department did away with buffalo by the hundreds. In 1995, the Montana legislature, bowing to the livestock industry's desire for more control over the Yellowstone bison, removed the species from FWP management and vested authority in the DOL. This was a problem for Dave, who was suddenly stripped of his state-sanctioned authority to kill. Ignoring his agency's new mandate, he continued to track and shoot buffalo, assisting the DOL during a winter when more than a thousand buffalo were slaughtered. He soon found himself without a job, but not for long, as the DOL hired him to locate and shoot buffalo the very next winter.

I met him during his first year as a DOL employee. I was out skiing a stretch of the Madison River, looking for buffalo, when Dave arrived on his DOL-issued snowmobile, clad in a black leather jacket. He had a high-powered rifle strapped to his back.

"Where are the buffalo?" he wanted to know.

"I'm not sure," I lied. "But I saw some elk a few miles back."

"I saw the tracks," he said shortly. "Now, why don't you tell me where they are?"

"So you can shoot them?" I asked.

"I'm not here to kill today," he said.

I glanced at his rifle. "Haven't seen them," I told him. "Maybe they went back to the park." Finding him more talkative than most of the agents I'd met, I decided to ask him some questions of my own: "Why do you care about bulls?" I pressed. "You know they can't transmit."

Wiping ice from his mustache, he ignored my question and asked one of his own. "Why don't you get a job?" Without waiting for an answer, he squeezed the throttle and sped off along the bluffs.

Dave's unwillingness to discuss the motives behind the bison slaughter is common among DOL agents. Although we sometimes find ourselves passing countless hours in the presence of the DOL, rarely will an agent enter into debate. Some say that they are following official policy in keeping tight-lipped, while others say they don't care to discuss it. Once in a while, an agent—bored, cold, or tired—will talk. Of the minority who do, most say that they're just doing a job, that they need the money. When pressed, they usually stick to brucellosis, Montana's official line.

The state blames brucellosis for the current slaughter, claiming that the presence of bison in Montana poses a grave economic threat to the livestock industry. Buffalo originally contracted brucellosis—a European livestock disease that can cause cattle cows to abort their first calves—from cows. Montana routinely argues that it has spent millions of dollars to eradicate the disease from its cattle in order to be certified as brucellosis-free by the United States Department of Agriculture (USDA). This certification allows livestock producers to export cattle without testing for brucellosis.

Federal regulations, however, don't justify the state's response. Montana can't lose its brucellosis-free status because wild animals are infected. Infection must occur among cattle. Even then, Montana would retain its brucellosis-free status until a second cattle herd became infected.

South of Yellowstone in Grand Teton National Park, where bison and livestock have coexisted for more than sixty years—and where a greater percentage of the bison herd is infected—bison have never transmited brucellosis to cattle. North of the park in 1989, more than 900 bison migrated across Yellowstone's north boundary and mingled with cattle near Gardiner. Fearing brucellosis transmission, the state tested 810 cattle from eighteen herds that had shared the range with bison and found no trace of the disease.

In a 1992 study, the United States Congress' General Accounting Office (GAO) concluded that Yellowstone's bison pose no threat of transmitting brucellosis to livestock. In its 1998 study, "Brucellosis in the Greater Yellowstone Ecosystem," the National Academy of Sciences concluded, "The current risk of transmission from YNP bison to cattle is low."

John Mack, a National Park Service wildlife biologist, concurs: "There is no evidence of wild, free-roaming bison transmitting brucellosis to cattle. The state is saying that this is a grave threat, and here you had all these bison mingle with livestock and nothing happened." Dr. Paul Nicolletti is a scientist widely respected for his work on brucellosis. In response to a question about the likelihood of transmission from Yellowstone bison to cattle, he responded, "The threat doesn't seem to be there."

Fear of disease transmission, despite the state's official line, isn't Montana's true impetus for killing buffalo. Brucellosis has been detected in many species, including elk, deer, moose, coyotes, wolves, bears, and bison. There are more than twenty times the number of elk than bison in the Yellowstone ecosystem, and elk have transmitted brucellosis to livestock, yet elk are allowed to roam freely between the park and Montana unmolested by the DOL. Writer Jay Kirkpatrick addresses Montana's double standard:

> It is public knowledge that wapiti (elk) test positive for brucellosis too, but that there is little concern about them destroying the cattle industry despite the fact that there are many times more wapiti than bison. These wapiti leave the park by the thousands and they share

private lands with cattle in the winter. Wapiti, however, represent a major industry in the state in the form of big game hunting, so they are tolerated.

Elk hunting is a major source of revenue for Montana, bringing in millions of dollars a year. My point is not to incite the livestock industry against elk but to note the inconsistency of Montana's logic. If brucellosis is such a grave threat, why is infection among the elk so blatantly ignored?

Brucellosis is a disease of the reproductive system. In order for buffalo to infect cattle, the cattle would have to eat placenta or the aborted fetus of an infected female buffalo. Bulls, nonpregnant cows, and calves—which don't shed such reproductive tissues—pose no risk. Because bison consume the afterbirth of their own offspring and rarely abort, even pregnant cows pose very little risk of infecting cattle. The Animal and Plant Health Inspection Service (APHIS), the USDA agency responsible for certifying a state as brucellosis-free, has stated that the presence of bulls and other low-risk bison such as calves and nonpregnant cows does not jeopardize Montana's brucellosis-free status. "We don't feel there's a need to kill every bison that comes out of the park," said APHIS spokesperson Patrick Collins in a reference to the DOL's intolerance for migrating bull bison.

Yet the state doesn't discriminate in its policy of killing bison wandering into Montana. During the winter of 1999, APHIS made public its objections to Montana's indiscriminate slaughter and assured the state that the presence of low-risk bison would not jeopardize Montana's brucellosis-free status. The DOL did not amend its policies in light of the APHIS objections. All bison, regardless of sex or age, continue to find themselves under the gun. Montana has killed hundreds of bulls since 1997.

West of the park bison and cattle do not come in contact with one another. Because cattle cannot survive the area's severe winters, ranchers graze them only from June to October, when the buffalo occupy their summer range inside Yellowstone. Even then, the number of cattle in the area is so small that it would be easy to ensure that they never come in contact with wandering bison. According to a recent report by the GAO, the investigative arm of Congress, "Only about 730 of the 2,000 cattle in the Greater Yellowstone area actually occupy lands that bison generally use when they leave the park." In 2013 the number is closer to 250. The brucella bacteria, which die in a few hours of exposure to direct sunlight, are not the driving force behind the state's zero-tolerance bison policy. It is a smoke screen for a policy that runs much deeper.

Viewing public support for the 1995 reintroduction of wolves into the Greater Yellowstone Ecosystem as a weathervane, the livestock industry fears a shift in public perceptions regarding management of federal lands. What's really at stake is the image, in the public eye, of bison reinhabiting any of their former range outside the park and competing with cattle for the limited range resource—grass. Brucellosis is a convenient excuse to kill bison.

Conducting research for the December 1997 issue of *National Parks* magazine, George Wuerthner interviewed an official working with the Wyoming Department of Game and Fish. The official, who asked to remain anonymous, told him that the issue boiled down to competition over grazing rights:

> *If the public gets used to the idea that bison, like elk and deer, should be free to roam on federal lands, then it may lead to a reduction in the amount of public lands forage allotted to livestock. That's what the ranchers really fear.*

John Varley, former director of the Yellowstone Center for Resources, also believes that the slaughter is driven by economics. In an article published in the May 1997 issue of *Audubon*, he calls the bison slaughter "a struggle between the park and agribusiness," a struggle which the park, he says, is "losing badly."

Wishing to sidestep a wildlife-versus-livestock debate over the best use of the public lands surrounding Yellowstone, the DOL launched a public relations campaign playing on Old West nostalgia and painting the Yellowstone bison as "diseased." The agency produced a colorful brochure with a cover photograph of a cowboy kneeling beside his son on the open range and teaching him to lasso cattle. Montana's famous big sky unfolds above, and a caption under the photo reads, "Oh, Give Me A Home, Where Disease-Free Buffalo Roam."

Although most DOL agents whom I've met are unwilling to discuss the reasoning behind the policies they enforce, occasionally one will admit that there is more to the slaughter than brucellosis. Last winter, an agent who had just spread a trail of hay from the park boundary into the bison trap told me it was population, not brucellosis, that his agency was controlling. "They'd be swimming in the sea if we weren't killing them when they leave the park," he said. According to this DOL employee, and others associated with Montana's livestock industry, bison are pests that should not be permitted to repopulate any of their former habitat adjacent to the park. One Idaho rancher who grazed cattle in the summer on Forest Service lands on Horse Butte believes that Yellowstone should be managed more like a zoo than as a functioning ecosystem. According to this rancher, "Bison belong in the park. They should keep them there."

DOL bison-slaughter operations protect not only the economic interests of cattle producers. Montana code actually provides a direct economic incentive for the agency to slaughter Yellowstone bison. A provision in Montana state law allows the DOL to credit its own accounts with the proceeds from the auction and sale of "diseased" bison. Title 81, chapter 2, section 120 of the Montana Code provides that the livestock "department . . . may sell a wild buffalo or bison carcass to help defray expenses of the department . . . the department shall deposit any revenue derived from the sale of the wild buffalo or bison carcass to the state special revenue fund to the credit of the department."

In 1997, the DOL held auctions, selling Yellowstone bison remains to the highest bidder. One 1997 auction netted the state $36,000. In January 1997, the state of Montana made more than $100,000 from the sale of bison meat, heads, and hides. Although the agency has not held an auction since 1997, it is still authorized to do so under the law.

I had plenty of time during my night in jail to question Montana's reasons for "lethal removal"—as they like to word it—of the only wild buffalo in the United States. Michael, my Floridian cell mate, was interested enough to listen. I told him the story as best I could, answering questions of my own as I tried to answer his. I had been learning to work with the media all winter, and most of my recent thoughts had been coming in a stream of sound bites and digital video. As I explained the situation to Michael, I took a step back and let myself feel the things I'd seen, slowing down to absorb the reality of the killing I had witnessed. I traced parallels between the slaughter of the nineteenth century and the contemporary killings, told him about the modern-day buffalo gunners, and tried to make sense of the brucellosis story. After I hinted at some of Montana's less visible reasons for killing buffalo, he began to understand why we would risk jail for the chance of keeping a few buffalo wild and alive. He was curious about the campaign and asked me how I had gotten involved.

I was working as an intern with a Missoula-based conservation group when I first heard about the campaign. In a situation common to the non-profit world, the executive director didn't know how to delegate authority and couldn't trust important tasks to anyone but himself. I worked in the office all fall, wondering what, if any, effects my work was having on the world. I was far removed from the wilds that I was supposedly helping to protect. When we started getting e-mails from a group of people living on the outskirts of West Yellowstone and running daily patrols along the park boundary, I became interested immediately. I had been researching the bison controversy since moving to Montana the previous winter when I learned of the slaughter of more than a thousand bison. After reading the first e-mail—a plea for volunteers to help with patrols—I responded at once, deciding to travel to Yellowstone over the holidays to help protect the buffalo.

Buffalo Field Campaign is headquartered in a large log cabin near the north shore of Hebgen Lake and provides room and board to those who volunteer for shifts in the field with the bison. Patrols stand vigil with the animals when they are outside the park, keeping them safe through a range of tactics from videography to civil disobedience. Every day that buffalo are outside the park, patrols are with them, ready to document or interfere should the DOL try to shoot or capture these herds.

I left Missoula in December 1997 planning on a weeklong trip to Yellowstone and ended up staying all winter. I arrived at the cabin on Christmas Eve, the day before my twenty-eighth birthday. As I drove up the snow-covered driveway toward the cabin on the hill, my stomach was a ball of knots. Overcome with a mixture of trepidation and eager anticipation, I felt like a child before the first day of school. I wondered who these people were and how I would fit in among them.

Perched in the foothills of the Madison Range with a view of Hebgen Lake, the large cabin had at one time served as a cross-country ski lodge. I walked up to the front of the building, climbed the steps to the porch, and was about to go inside when a kid in his late teens came out the front door and introduced himself. "You must be the guy from Missoula," he said. "I'm Peaches."

As I would soon learn, many of the activists went by what they called "forest names," names that could be used among activists but couldn't be traced back to social security numbers or arrest warrants by law-enforcement officers paid to monitor or identify activists. I met folks with names like Chipmunk, Echo, Mango, Slug, Grumble, Frog, Willow, Felony, Smoosh, Festus, Snowflake, Locust, and Turtle. Others chose to go by their given names. Some tried to come up with names for themselves, but if a name didn't fit, it wouldn't stick. Peaches, it turned out, was new to his forest name when I met him. One night, before he was Peaches, some folks around the cabin were joking about how he needed a new name. "You guys can call me Vern," he told them. "Just don't call me Peaches." He's been Peaches ever since.

"If you're hungry, there's some soup and bread in the kitchen," he said. "The pot's on the stove."

"Thanks," I told him, and then I stepped inside. I met Grace in the front hallway, a small room stuffed with shelves of boots and racks of coats. "You must be Dan," she said. "It's good you came when you did. We've been losing volunteers all week. Lots of folks have taken off for Christmas."

I followed her into the living room, a large room with sleeping lofts built in the rafters. The walls on three sides were lined with Goodwill couches; a giant woodstove dominated the fourth. The basil-garlic scent of the homemade soup reminded me of my mother's kitchen. I followed my nose, found a bowl, and ladled myself some of the thick lentil soup, then broke off a chunk of bread from a French loaf and sat on a wooden bench to warm myself before the stove. "I'll be in the office," Grace said. "Come find me after you've eaten and I'll show you around."

As I ate, several people came into the room and introduced themselves. "I'm Eric," said a lanky kid whom I recognized. An upstate New Yorker by birth, he had been traveling across the country until he found Montana and fell in love with the mountains. I had met him two months earlier in the Missoula office. He had come in asking if I knew of any groups needing volunteers. "I'm tired of moving around so much," he told me. "I'm ready to give something back to this place." Having just received my first e-mail, I told him about the buffalo campaign being organized near West Yellowstone.

He recognized me. "Oh yeah, you're the guy from Missoula," he said. "I'm glad you made it down here. We could use more people."

"How many are here?" I asked him.

"I think there are twelve now, with you here," he said.

I finished my soup and found Grace in the office. She was answering e-mails on an old Mac. "We get about fifty a day," she told me. "We try to answer them all, but it's impossible. You're dead tired when you get in from patrol. The last thing you feel like doing is staring into a screen."

I took a look around. On a table in one corner there were two three-quarter-inch video decks and several Sony video cameras. A bumper sticker plastered to the wall above the table read, "The Camcorder is Mightier than the Baton." Grace noticed me looking at the cameras and said, "Those are our most powerful tools. If the DOL knows their every move is recorded, they won't be nearly as reckless." On the wall above the decks was a gruesome color photo of four severed bison heads lying in the snow. Blood dripped from the nostrils and pooled around the necks, contrasting with the white background. On another table stood four two-way FM walkie-talkies.

During the next few days I learned the routine. Wake up at 5:30, eat a good breakfast prepared by Grumbles, gear up, and get out the door by 6 A.M. I took to the ski shifts at Duck Creek, with its beautiful sunrises, right away. Most mornings this valley teems with wildlife. Herds of elk 200 strong standing against a backdrop of seventy buffalo are a frequent treat at sunrise by the creek. Occasionally we are honored with the presence of gray wolves and coyotes pacing the periphery of the great herds.

The buffalo appear every fall, trickling from the park along the path of least resistance following the drainages of Duck Creek, Cougar Creek, and the Madison River. When winter turns fierce and snow obscures the grass from which their bodies are built, bison pour out, migrating down the watercourses to lower elevations outside the park. Theirs is often a one-way migration, as they are killed when they follow their instincts into Montana.

The DOL keeps a bison trap in the primary migration corridor between Yellowstone and the surrounding Gallatin National Forest. The trap, on land abutting the park boundary, sits less than a hundred feet from Duck Creek. The land is owned by a man who leases it to the DOL. He shares his house with DOL agents, and they keep their snowmobiles, tractors, and other equipment in his barn. He owns property on both sides of the creek. Every winter, when the snow begins to build in the park, hundreds of buffalo migrate through this man's land on their way to their winter habitat on Horse Butte. He and the DOL entice hungry bison onto the property by placing bales of hay near the park boundary.

In September 1999, Buffalo Field Campaign volunteers found the carcass of a bull bison on the boundary of this person's property. The dead bull had been stripped of its head, hide, and genitals. The volunteers notified the FWP, who launched an investigation. When the property owner was initially questioned about the incident, he denied any knowledge of or involvement in the shooting. Only after the head and cape were discovered in his possession did he claim responsibility. He told investigators that the bison was "bothering" his truck. At his trial, he defended his actions by saying, "Buffalo aren't worth much. There are plenty of them. When my truck was in danger, too bad for the buffalo."

His lawyer attempted to have the charges dismissed on the grounds that buffalo are "vermin." At the pretrial hearing, the property owner told the judge, "Buffalo are unregulated vermin in Montana and have the same status as gophers, which are shot up by the buckets full each spring." He was acquitted on the charge of illegal hunting and convicted for illegally possessing a game animal. He was fined $320.

Because of its importance as a migration corridor and because it serves as DOL headquarters and houses one of their traps, this man's property is watched closely by Buffalo Field Campaign patrols. In the fall and early winter, when large concentrations of buffalo are moving out of the park, two patrols are assigned to the Duck Creek area. The Fir Ridge patrol, named after the ridge to the north of the creek from where the skiers drop into the valley, is a backcountry patrol that monitors the land between the buffalo trap and Yellowstone. The Duck Creek patrol is a car shift that roves up and down Duck Creek Road, watching the property owner's driveway for DOL activity and monitoring the property from an overlook known among volunteers as "The Perch."

Our job on these early mornings is to survey this man's land and make sure that no buffalo have wandered onto it during the night. The Fir Ridge and Duck Creek patrols work together and communicate via two-way radio. The perch offers a bird's-eye view of the property owner's yard and the trap, a different view than the one the skiers get from the boundary. If buffalo enter this man's land during the night, skiers sometimes move in at first light and attempt to shepherd them back to Yellowstone. The DOL arrests anyone caught trespassing on the property owner's land.

Four days after I arrived at the cabin, I participated in an action and helped save sixteen buffalo. Peaches, on his way home from work in town the night before, had seen two DOL trucks pull into the property owner's yard. Because they were towing livestock trailers (used to transport captured bison to slaughter), we believed that they were in town to capture buffalo.

The next morning, Eric, Grace, and I woke extra early, ate a hasty oatmeal breakfast in silence, and left the cabin an hour before sunrise. I parked the car by the Fir Ridge cemetery. We stepped into our skis in the frosty dawn and followed the well-packed trail toward the park, reaching the top of Fir Ridge well before sunrise. A porch light was on at the man's home.

I took four sweeping strides and shot off the ridge, plunging into the darkness below. My skis slid smoothly, humming in the icy tracks. I bent my knees and shifted my weight forward, flying down the hill, taking as much speed as I could for my glide across the valley floor. We skied onto a small bluff overlooking the buffalo trap and stood on the property line, watching the man's house and barn. A few minutes after we arrived, a light came on in the house.

Eric fumbled through his pack for a walkie-talkie, held it before his mouth, pressed the button, and said, "Backcountry to perch, do you copy?"

A voice came through. "This is perch. You see anything down there? Over."

"Not yet," Eric replied. "Just got here. The porch light went on. We're waiting for a touch of sun to reveal our friends. Over."

While they were talking, Grace skied farther along the bluff. She came back a few minutes later and said she'd spotted them. "They're right next to his house," she said.

They spotted them from the perch, too: "We have sixteen of our friends practically sitting on the porch. DOL is up and about. Looks like it's now or never."

"We better get going," Grace said. "It's almost light." Eric and I agreed. He waited on the bluff with the radio while she and I skied in. We pushed past a row of fence posts and skied beside the trap and into a grove of trees, the only cover on the property. Stopping at the edge of the grove, we surveyed the scene. The buffalo were bedded down on a small rise behind a fence, fifteen feet from the property owner's front door. A mound of hay had been placed beside the porch.

"That's why they like it here so much," Grace said. "They're luring them in with hay."

Human shadows shifted in the house. "We'd better do it or we'll be caught in daylight," I whispered. Grace nodded and said, "Let's go." Pushing with my poles and sprinting on my skis, I closed the distance to the house. This was the closest I had ever been to buffalo, and I was amazed at their immensity. Giving the buffalo plenty of room and skiing to within five feet of the house, I pulled the ski mask over my face and passed before the sliding glass door. I wasn't afraid of being gored so much as I was of being arrested by the DOL, for even as we woke the sleeping giants and coaxed them toward the park, I could feel that they somehow sensed our intentions.

"Hayyaa!! Hayyaa!!" I whisper-shouted, clacking my poles together and jumping up and down. The buffalo reacted quickly, rising to their feet. Several of the bulls hopped a small fence and moved toward the park. Most trotted around it and ambled in the tracks of the leaders. I moved quickly, trying to stay close enough to keep them moving yet not too close, because I didn't want them to double back around me. As we moved slowly to the east with the buffalo, crossing the invisible park boundary, human voices called us from the property owner's home as DOL agents realized, too late, what was going on. Because they don't ski and their snowmobiles are not allowed in the park's backcountry, the agents couldn't chase us. We didn't linger to heed their commands.

We meandered slowly up the creek, giving the buffalo plenty of room. They lumbered through the heavy snow single file, the one in front breaking trail for those behind. This is a technique we used as well, taking turns to break trail as we skied or snowshoed across snow-covered meadows. When the bull in front grew tired, he stepped off the trail, allowing the herd to pass and the one behind him to break for awhile.

As we skied behind them, I caught sight of a coyote across the valley. She eyed us as we made our way beside the trickling creek. When we reached a sharp oxbow, the buffalo plunged over the bank, splashed across the channel, and hauled their bodies to the opposite side. The last two bulls turned slowly and stared at us before joining the others in a sheltered meadow where tufts of grass poked through the snow.

We sat on our packs and watched them graze across the valley as the sun pulled itself free of the mountains in the park. I took a pair of binoculars from my pack and trained them on the grazing bison. A huge bull, the largest of the group, nearly filled the field of vision. He buried his face in the snow and swung his head from side to side, nuzzling a crater in the snow and exposing a patch of grass. He lifted his broad, snow-covered face in my direction and chomped, a sheaf of grass hanging from his lips.

Grace and Eric said that they were getting wet and cold and wanted to take a warming ski. I had a head full of thoughts and wasn't ready to leave the meadow. We made plans to meet by the graveyard in two hours, and my friends skied away. My gaze moved easily from the backs of the buffalo to the mountains in the park. Studying the rise and fall of peaks on a nearby ridge, I realized how much they resembled the bull's silhouette with its gently rising back, steep, peaked hump, valley of a neck, and rounded head. I stared back and forth, marveling at how perfectly the buffalo fit their surroundings and how well adapted they are at surviving Yellowstone's difficult winters.

Gradually my thoughts drifted to the coming winter. I was supposed to leave in two days to return to my office internship in Missoula. Staring east, into Yellowstone, I remembered the morning in the park, five years earlier, when my mother came to speak to me in a dream. Watching the buffalo graze against the backdrop of Yellowstone's mountains, I thought about how different the day might have turned out. I saw the sixteen bison confined inside the trap. I remembered my mother's voice, "The path you are on is right. I am with you." Her words echoed in my head, dissolving any remaining doubt. I wasn't going back to Missoula.

❦

With the campaign, I was in my element, drawing on many of the skills I'd developed during my twenties. I worked in the office, fielding calls and e-mail inquiries, writing press releases, and speaking to reporters. I learned to shoot and edit video and coproduced *Buffalo Bull*, a fifty-minute documentary. Around the cabin, my carpentry skills were in high demand, as the ever-increasing number of volunteers required the construction of sleeping lofts and shelves for gear. Most rewarding was the time I was able to spend outside, along the boundary on patrol in the presence of buffalo. On skis every day, monitoring migrations and standing vigil with the herds, I began to develop a relationship with the buffalo, learning their habits and how to tell when they felt threatened and defensive. I learned how to observe them from a respectful distance and how to coax them to move when they were in danger.

Although I wasn't being paid in legal tender, I was earning the best living of my life. All necessities were provided: inspiring work, a group of friends who believed in something enough to act in its defense—putting their lives and freedom on the line in the process—delicious meals, and a warm cabin for shelter. Although it gets quite crowded at times, the place always feels like home.

I have spent thirteen winters with Buffalo Field Campaign. Since I first walked in the door in December 1997, more than 4,000 volunteers have come from across the country and around the world. Each was motivated by a unique set of circumstances, and each went away a different person than when he or she came. Hearing their stories and getting to know them are among the most rewarding aspects of being involved with the campaign. Under the cabin roof, I have had discussions with factory workers, bankers, teachers, county planners, park rangers, filmmakers, high-school dropouts, computer technicians, and seasoned activists—all united in the common cause of keeping Yellowstone wild and its bison alive. These people, all called in one way or another by the buffalo, sacrificed time with their families, friends, and jobs to lend a hand.

Being a Buffalo Field Campaign volunteer involves more than skiing in the park. It requires days on end of rising before the sun and going out in subfreezing weather and braving fierce winter storms and temperatures as low as minus fifty degrees Fahrenheit. It means sitting in the snow for days, waiting for something to happen. When it does happen, you wish it hadn't, because animals you've been watching for months are suddenly and violently disrupted—chased with snowmobiles, helicopters, and gunshots—trapped in steel cages, poked and prodded, squeezed in chutes, tested, and killed. It means participating in seemingly endless meetings, deciding the next day's strategy. And for more than seventy volunteers, it has meant sacrificing freedom and spending time behind bars.

My arrest occurred during the campaign's second winter, in March 1999, when Pete and I followed four bulls away from the Duck Creek trap. More than eighty bison were backed up on the park line as our around-the-clock patrols attempted to keep them away from the hay that had been piled on the private property to lure them in. When we reached Horse Butte, Mike—one of the campaign's cofounders—and Jessie, a teenage volunteer who had recently arrived, joined us. The four of us were walking behind the four bulls along a Forest Service road when four DOL agents pulled up on their snowmobiles from the other direction, blocking our path. The road, which hadn't been cleared all winter, had been plowed for the first time earlier in the day. As a result, it was bound by nearly vertical snowbanks ten feet high. One of the agents taunted, "Where do you think you're going with them bulls?" We all held our ground, three sets of four. The bulls, weighing a ton apiece and capable of running thirty miles an hour, paced in circles between the livestock agents and the four activists. We knew that, if we left, the agents would chase them back to the trap. We backed off just a bit to give the bulls more room. Suddenly they surprised us, doing what none of us thought possible. In a matter of seconds, they broke the tension, trotting up and over the ten-foot snowbank and bypassing the agents. We followed in their tracks, ecstatic, to make sure that they were safe. As it turned out, the agents were more interested in capturing us than the buffalo.

After trailing the bulls to an area away from the road, we left them to graze in peace. As we approached the agents, we agreed to keep quiet and not taunt them about their failure to stop the bulls. When we passed them, stepping in buffalo tracks on the snow berm, they were still sitting on their sleds in the road. We stuck to our pledge until we were twenty feet past them. Pete couldn't resist. He turned around and teased, "Nice try, boys. Maybe next time." Before I knew what was happening, Pete was facedown in the snow beside the road, tackled and pinned by an agent. After cuffing

Pete's hands behind his back, the agent and the others turned their attention to Mike and then to Jessie, handcuffing them and leaving them standing in the snow. I walked up to Jessie and took the radio from his pocket, called the cabin, and told them what was happening, then went to Mike for the video camera, which hung from his neck.

The agent told me at least three times that I was not under arrest and was free to go. When I asked him what my friends were being charged with, he wouldn't talk. I kept asking, camera rolling, and finally he mumbled something about trespassing. I reminded him that we were in the Gallatin National Forest, public land on which we had every right to be. A little while later I stepped into the road, meaning to cross it for a better camera angle. I wanted a shot of my handcuffed friends in the custody of the cattle inspectors against a backdrop of the Madison Range. "Stop right there!" the agent shouted. "This road is closed to the public." This was the first I had heard of the closure, and I questioned his authority, an agent of the state of Montana, to close a road belonging to all Americans.

"How am I supposed to get to my car?" I asked. He pointed toward a cattle guard a quarter mile down the road. "You can cross down there." I followed his directions and returned to the arrest scene on the other side of the road. I could have walked away at that point but decided to stay, not wanting to leave my friends alone with the agents without the protection of the video camera. An hour after Pete's arrest, several sheriffs' deputies arrived and conferred with the DOL agents. As they huddled to plan their strategy, the officers kept turning their heads, sizing me up, and I knew I was done for. I stood and started away, making only three steps before a deputy yelled, "Hold it right there. You're under arrest!"

We were transported ninety miles to Bozeman and put in jail. I was separated from my friends and locked in a small cell, where I met Michael Ray. I wasn't booked until 4 A.M., nine hours after the arrest. All four of us were cited with misdemeanor violations. The tickets read: "Negligent Endangerment to wit: By herding buffalo, which created substantial risk of death or serious bodily injury to Department of Livestock Officers." The conditions of our release stipulated that we couldn't set foot within 1,500 feet of any DOL operation, both buffalo traps, and most of the Horse Butte Peninsula. A generous local citizen who learned of our arrest from a newspaper article put up the $2,000 bail required for our release.

Banned from the field, I spent more time in the office writing press releases and articles, editing video footage, and communicating with supporters. While this was necessary work, it was difficult to remain cabin-bound while my friends spent their days out on skis with the buffalo. I listened to their stories at the nightly meetings, wishing I could make more of a contribution. It was during this time, bound to the office, that I began organizing my thoughts for this book.

Because we had captured on videotape the events preceding the arrests, we asked for jury trials. The tape contained strong evidence showing that we had not attempted to injure the agents. Two days before the trial, my charges were dismissed. My three friends had their charges dropped as well. Such heavy-handed tactics—making false accusations and asking for bail restrictions to limit our ability to protect the buffalo—have been a favorite tactic of the DOL ever since.

I'll always be haunted by memories of buffalo being forced through narrow chutes inside the Duck Creek trap, men poised above them shouting "Yee-hauw!" as they hit them with shovels swung like golf clubs. Even now I can hear the chaotic clang of steel as the frantic bison thrust themselves against the trap's cold, steel walls, aching to return to a world they have known for tens of thousands of years.

With these memories come thoughts of my night in jail and of my cell mate, Michael. His questions and my attempts at answering helped me realize the importance of putting my stories down in words. I often think of Michael's crazy misconception of Yellowstone as a gated zoo for a few wild animals. I wonder how he felt as he stood inside the Grizzly Discovery Center, staring at the bears in their cells, believing he was in Yellowstone. After five winters of bearing witness to the DOL's treatment of America's only wild bison herd—keeping them in the park with a fence of bullets or luring them to death with hay—I am beginning to understand how he must have felt.

three

Inseparable Destiny

In life and death we and the buffalo have always shared the same fate.

—John Fire Lame Deer

The fear of wilderness, the fear of indigenous people, and the fear of not having control are all the same fear.
—Linda Hogan

G RANDMA, HOW OLD DO YOU HAVE TO BE TO GET ARRESTED?" Timothy asks Rosalie. They are standing between a county road and a barbed-wire fence, staring out past the fence to an open field. Eight dead buffalo, bodies still warm, litter the meadow. Never shifting her gaze from her slain siblings, Rosalie Little Thunder reaches into her bag for the sage bundle and steps around the fence. Crossing the field to pray over the bodies, she is approached by a sheriff's deputy, who tells her she'll be arrested for criminal trespass if she doesn't leave immediately. "Mitakuye Oyasin," she says, beginning her prayer. Grabbing her arms and squeezing handcuffs around her wrists, the deputy leads the Lakota elder to the white Explorer and locks her inside.

"Mitakuye Oyasin" is a Lakota phrase meaning "all my relations." It is used to invoke not only blood relatives and close friends but, as the Lakota say, all two-legged people, four-legged people, crawling and swimming people, winged people, and people with roots. This powerful prayer expresses recognition of not just living relatives, but those who have come through this world before us and passed into the one beyond. By beginning her prayers with "Mitakuye Oyasin," Rosalie shows respect for the interrelationship between all beings and events, past, present, and future.

Witnessing the dead buffalo and the DOL agents who killed them (they laughed as she prayed) reminded Rosalie of the tragic family stories she'd heard her grandparents tell. A direct descendant of survivors of both the 1855 Little Thunder Massacre and the nefarious Sand Creek Massacre of 1864, Rosalie felt like she was reliving history as she and her ten-year-old grandson watched the agents gloat over the eight slain bison.

After a delegation of Cheyenne and Arapaho leaders attended peace talks with US and Colorado officials, the Indians were promised protection by military leaders if they agreed to camp near Fort Lyon on Sand Creek. Trusting the officials, more than 500 Cheyennes and Arapahos, and a few of their Sioux allies—including Rosalie's ancestors—set up their tipis where the soldiers had advised them to camp. Colonel John Chivington, commanding 600 inexperienced soldiers of the Colorado Third Cavalry, attacked shortly after sunrise on November 29, 1864. Black Kettle, the Cheyenne leader who had attended the peace talks, raised a large American flag from a tall pole before his lodge. But the soldiers were following orders: Take no prisoners.

Three columns of troops marched up the creek, one in the bed and one on each of the banks. They killed everyone in their path. The Indians fled, many running up the creek ahead of the soldiers. Digging quick pits in the creek bank, they climbed in, hunkered down, and attempted to defend themselves. One woman fled up the creek with her small boy beside her and her baby on her back. When she reached the safety of the pits, she discovered that her baby, still strapped to her back, had been shot. Her husband, too, had been killed. After firing on the pits for more than four hours, then scalping heads and dismembering bodies, the soldiers left. After dark, the few survivors pulled themselves from the potholes and disappeared into the night.

Proud soldiers marched triumphantly through downtown Denver. Between acts of a theatrical performance, playgoers were treated to a display of more than 100 scalps, held high above the stage by beaming soldiers.

Chivington bragged: "We killed between four and five hundred Indians. Our loss is nine killed and thirty-eight wounded. All did nobly." Other sources report that 150 Indians were killed. Two-thirds of the dead were women and children.

Gruesome testimony to the soldiers' atrocities surfaced in the ensuing investigation. One Cheyenne woman was partially scalped but not killed. People saw her running around blindly, a flap of forehead skin dangling in front of her eyes. Another witness described a scene in which a soldier, hoping to spare the lives of three children—ranging in age from four to eight—brought them to the attention of a lieutenant. The commanding officer coldly responded, "Orders are to kill small and big," which is what Chivington had reportedly told his officers before the attack. Then the officer shot one of the children in the head with his pistol. Ignoring their pleas for mercy, he raised his gun slowly, shot the second child, reloaded, and then killed the last.

Rosalie's own grandfather had survived similar horrors a decade before Sand Creek, in 1855. At the age of ten, he was camped with his family, the Little Thunder band, near the North Platte River in present-day Nebraska. Their rights to the land on which they were camped had been acknowledged by the US government with the signing of the first Fort Laramie Treaty in 1851. Ignoring provisions of the treaty, US troops led by General Harney attacked the peaceful village. In a series of events that would be mirrored by Black Kettle at Sand Creek, Chief Little Thunder flew a white flag as General Harney and his troops descended upon the village.

A woman stood with her ten-year-old grandson on the edge of camp near some bushes and tall grass. She watched as Chief Little Thunder met the advancing troops under the white flag of truce. As the general and the chief exchanged words, she told her grandson to hide in a burrow near her feet. "Stay here—don't come out yet," she told him. As soon as she had concealed him with her shawl, the soldiers opened fire. Struck by a bullet, the woman threw her body down on the shawl, concealing her small grandson. The boy remained motionless in his dark hole as his grandmother's blood soaked through her shawl and dripped down on him. After nightfall, he climbed past her cold body and traveled north, toward the Black Hills, 200 miles away.

"That little boy, he was my grandfather," Rosalie said as she explained how it felt, the day of her arrest, to stand with her grandson and witness the slaughter of eight buffalo at the hands of grinning government agents:

> It was that déja vu feeling that you've been here before . . . that's what that whole scene was when they were killing the buffalo. That was what was coming back to me. I had my ten-year-old grandson standing next to me. And they started killing the buffalo, just like that, shooting them down. I covered his face with my shawl and told him not to move.

Rosalie, her grandson Timothy Kills in Water, and tribal members from across the plains assembled near Gardiner, Montana, on March 7, 1997, to hold a prayer ceremony for the Yellowstone buffalo. More than 1,000 had been killed in the preceding months. The sanctity of the ceremony, attended by spiritual leaders from various tribes, was shattered by the violence of rifle fire as DOL agents gunned down eight buffalo just a mile away. To Rosalie, who was arrested when she left the ceremony to investigate the shots, the DOL's timing was intentional. "They shot those buffalo because we were at that place on that day at that time," she said.

As close as I hold the beautiful, sacred buffalo to my heart, I can't begin to fathom the depths of what Rosalie must have felt that day at having been so disrespected and abused. To the Lakota, and to other plains tribes, nothing is more sacred than the buffalo. Arvol Looking Horse, a traditional Lakota spiritual leader who led the prayer that day, noted that the Yellowstone bison are special because they, like Indians, are "survivors of an apocalypse."

The current slaughter of the Yellowstone buffalo, the most wild buffalo left in America, is seen by many as a deliberate attempt on the part of government agencies to disempower native peoples. To many Native Americans, particularly those inhabiting the once-buffalo-rich western plains, the fate of the buffalo and the fate of the people have always been inseparable. Fred Dubray, a Lakota who lives on the Cheyenne River Reservation, expresses awareness of this connection:

> *It was so difficult for European people to understand that they feared that relationship that existed, and what they fear, they destroy. So, that's exactly what started to happen. For thousands of years these buffalo have had a very intimate relationship with tribal people. We are the same. As a matter of fact, if you go back in time a little bit, our legends and our stories, creation stories say that we are the same, we come from exactly the same place. No matter how hard you try, you can't separate Indian people from buffalo. That is not even possible.*

The belief that people and buffalo originated together inside the earth is expressed in the creation accounts of many plains tribes. The Lakota share with neighboring tribes the recognition that their lives are deeply intertwined with the lives of the buffalo. Although similar stories could be drawn from any number of Plains tribes, there are four that I want to highlight.

Scott Frazier, a member of the Crow tribe with both Santee and Crow ancestry, introduced us to plains creation accounts when he recounted the Santee creation at one of Buffalo Field Campaign's nightly meetings. The story illustrates the genesis of the sacred human–buffalo relationship and the original sacrifice that the buffalo made for human beings.

> *The story begins after the world was formed but when the people still lived inside the world. The buffaloes were sacred and we tended them. We fed them a food that was like clouds. The life we had was sacred, but some of the people wanted to see what lay outside the tunnel to the surface. One of those who decided to go up the tunnel was named To ka hey, "the first one." He went to the surface to look around. He came back with wonderful stories. The people were curious but decided not to let on that they were going to the surface. Seven families left. Soon*

the buffaloes realized what had happened. They went to the surface.
What they saw was sad. The people had nothing to eat; they were cold
and without shelter. Those buffaloes decided that although the people
had been foolish, the buffaloes needed to go to the surface and help the
people. The buffaloes knew that if they went to the surface they could
not return to the life they knew within the earth. The buffaloes gave up
their life within the earth so that the people could have food, clothing,
and shelter. What they did was holy.

According to the Pawnee version, all creatures, not just humans and the great herds of buffalo, but antelope, coyotes, wolves, elk, deer, rabbits, and birds originated together, deep underground, as if asleep. Buffalo Woman awoke and started walking past the other animals and people. She walked to a dark, round place and stood still, looking straight ahead. Then she bowed her head as one who is passing under a lodge flap does. For an instant she was framed in blinding light; then she was gone.

A small buffalo cow got up and followed her, then another buffalo, and another. She was soon trailing a long thread of buffaloes. Each one crossed the threshold in a brilliant burst of light. After the last buffalo, the people were on their feet and following. They found a warm and fertile prairie, a world of beautiful, green grass with the Platte River at its center. The people looked up and saw the blue sky above it all, as they felt, for the first time, the sun upon their faces. They watched the buffalo spread across the prairie, feeding as they walked, heading out in every direction. They knew that they had found their home, a place where they and the buffalo would always belong.

Plenty Coups describes a vision in which he witnessed the creation of his people, the Crow:

> *Out of the hole in the ground came the buffalo, bulls and*
> *cows and calves without number. They spread wide and black-*
> *ened the plains. Everywhere I looked great herds of buffalo*

were going in every direction, and still others without num-
ber were pouring out of the hole in the ground to travel on the
wide plains.

Like other plains tribes, the Lakota creation stories take place underground with buffalo. Wind Cave, in the Black Hills, is the doorway through
which the Lakota followed the buffalo into the world. Greg Bourland, of the
Cheyenne River Sioux tribe, described the Lakota creation story at a recent
public hearing on bison management:

> *Prior to coming and living on this earth, as we know it today, we*
> *lived with the buffalo. Together we lived in the land beneath the earth,*
> *and the trickster told us that the earth was really a good place. Well,*
> *trickster had been living up here tricking the animals, and he wanted us*
> *up here so he could have new beings to fool. But when we came upon*
> *the earth, we realized the earth was a hard place in which to live. Our*
> *job down in the other world had been to take care of the buffalo people.*
> *And so when we came onto the earth, the buffalo people felt sorry for*
> *us. They took pity upon us, and in that pity, they came up onto the*
> *earth and became the buffalo. And they took care of us. They provided*
> *us with their hide for clothing, for shelter, for the things that we would*
> *need to survive. Their flesh for food, their bones for tools.*

Like their relatives the Santee, the Lakota sustained the buffalo in the
earth. The relationship reversed only after they passed into this world. After
watching the people starve on earth, the buffalo decided to sacrifice their
lives so that the people could survive. These creation accounts reveal the origins of the buffalo and the people, and they explain the origins of the sacred
human–buffalo relationship.

For the Lakota, this is the most important relationship. As John Fire
Lame Deer eloquently explains, the connections between his people and the
buffalo are so strong that it can be difficult to distinguish one from the other:

The buffalo was part of us, his flesh and blood being absorbed by us until it became our own flesh and blood. Our clothing, our tipis, everything we needed for life came from the buffalo's body. It was hard to say where the animal ended and the man began.

Buffalo lent themselves to virtually every aspect of Lakota life. Hides made warm clothing, tipi covers, saddles, reins, ropes, and water bags. Flesh was eaten fresh or dried into jerky so that it would keep. Bones made knives, needles, awls, clubs, and sled runners. A red-hot stone was dropped in the buffalo's stomach for a self-contained stove and kettle. The skull was used as a sacred altar or in ceremonies.

The centrality of the buffalo to the lives of the equestrian nomadic tribes of the plains wasn't lost on nineteenth-century military leaders and politicians. General Sheridan knew that a people were only as strong as their food source. He believed that the buffalo should be eradicated to pacify the few remaining Indians who refused to relinquish their lives to the ways of the whites:

If I could learn that every buffalo in the northern herd were killed I would be glad. The destruction of this herd would do more to keep Indians quiet than anything else that could happen.

Government and military leaders shared Sheridan's views. Interior Secretary Columbus Delano lobbied for buffalo eradication in his 1872 annual report:

The civilization of the Indian is impossible while the buffalo remains upon the plains. . . . I would not seriously regret the total disappearance of the buffalo from our western prairies, in its effect upon the Indians, regarding it as a means of hastening their sense of dependence upon the products of the soil and their own labors.

In 1876, US Representative James Throckmorton argued that the mere presence of buffalo posed an obstacle to the advancement of Euro-American civilization:

> *There is no question that, so long as there are millions of buffaloes in the West, the Indians cannot be controlled, even by the strong arm of the Government. I believe it would be a great step forward in the civilization of the Indians and the preservation of peace on the border if there was not a buffalo in existence.*

The politicians in Washington and the military men in the field exploited the close connections between the buffalo and the Indians, encouraging the destruction of one to defeat the other. Army officers violated legal treaties, allowing white hunters to trespass onto tribal lands that had been set aside to exclusive Indian use. The Medicine Lodge Treaties of 1867 prohibited whites from hunting south of the Arkansas River. Hunting rights there were supposed to be reserved for the Arapahoes, Cheyennes, Comanches, and Kiowas. At a time when the buffalo population was suffering a major and rapid decline, the infamous buffalo runner J. Wright Mooar was eager to pursue his prey on the restricted lands. He and other hunters asked Colonel Richard Dodge what the penalty would be if they should disregard the law and cross the line. Dodge reportedly told them, "Boys, if I were a buffalo hunter, I would hunt where the buffalo are."

This discrimination against Native American nations through the slaughter of buffalo has resumed. The DOL's slaughter of eight bison as Rosalie Little Thunder and other tribal members performed their ceremonies is testimony to the reemergence of a centuries-old pattern of government disregard for tribal rights. The slaughter, an attack on the religion and culture of the Plains Indians, grows out of one culture's disrespect for the beliefs of another. Chasing Hawk of the Cheyenne River Sioux tribe makes this clear:

> *We are the buffalo people, the Lakota People. When they kill [the Yellowstone] buffalo, they are killing our brothers and sisters, grandpas*

and grandmas. The State of Montana did not see this. In fact, our religious significance is nothing to them.

The deep familial relationship between the buffalo and human beings is, for many tribes, as old as time itself. When Chasing Hawk describes the buffalo as brothers and sisters, he isn't speaking metaphorically. The buffalo living in and around present-day Yellowstone National Park are the last living remnants of the wild herds that once sustained Chasing Hawk's ancestors. To kill these buffalo is to discriminate against the plains tribes.

At the root of the buffalo slaughter lies a clash of cultures. The dominant Euro-American worldview holds that nonhuman animals aren't entitled to the same rights as humans. Human comfort comes before animal survival. To the Lakota and other plains tribes, the notion of "people" encompasses more than the human race. Buffalo are people. Agreements have been worked out since the earliest days when people and buffalo shared life inside the earth and the buffalo made the original sacrifice for the humans. These agreements are renewed every year through seasonal reenactments like the Sundance, a ceremony through which people sacrifice their bodies to the buffalo.

When DOL agents, who knew about the prayer ceremony, slaughtered eight buffalo and arrested Rosalie Little Thunder, it sent a clear message to Native Americans across the plains. Rosalie thinks of the incident as "a murder in the church parking lot, during the service." She and other elders who experienced the day's events view them as a renewed attack against her people. There is little difference, she has said, between the nineteenth-century slaughter of buffalo and the slaughter of their descendants today.

The essence of the sacred relationship between the Lakota Nation and the Buffalo Nation is manifest in the sacred Lakota pipe bundle. White Buffalo Calf Woman, who had the power to change herself from a young woman to a white buffalo calf, brought the pipe to the people as a symbol of the sacred human–buffalo kinship and to show them the proper ways to respect that kinship. She taught them ceremonies to honor and renew the relationship. She told the people to offer the pipe to the Great Spirit when there was no food, and the buffalo would come. If they cared for the pipe in the proper manner, the pipe would warn them of impending trouble. After leaving the sacred pipe with the Lakota, she walked away singing, "Niya taniya mawani ye," which has been translated as, "With visible breath I am walking." It means that as long as they honor the pipe, they will live, will remain themselves. And the thought of "visible breath" can be taken as the smoke of the pipe, which is the breath of their people. It also reminds them of the breath of the buffalo as it can be seen on a cold day. It underlines the fact that, for the Lakota, the pipe, human beings, and the buffalo are all one.

The Lakota maintain the pipe to this day, following the original instructions passed down through sixteen generations. When Lakota spiritual leaders traveled to Montana in March 1997 to pray for the 1,084 buffalo slaughtered that winter, they prayed with this sacred pipe. Arvol Looking Horse, seventeenth-generation keeper of the pipe, led the ceremony. During the prayer, he asked for respect from other nations and expressed the importance of the buffalo to the Lakota way of life: "I humbly ask all nations to respect our way of life, because in our prophecies, if there are no buffalo, then life as we know it will cease to exist."

The DOL's decision to open fire during the Lakota ceremony was, at best, deeply disrespectful. At worst, it was a premeditated act of violence directed at those who had come to pray for their relatives, the buffalo. Whatever the reason they chose to kill the eight buffalo and arrest Rosalie during the ceremony, their intention wasn't to create a movement. But the power of the prayer, focused through the sacred pipe, set powerful forces in motion that day.

The ceremony organized by Looking Horse and Little Thunder was an event of historical, as well as spiritual, significance. Since 1990, videographers with the Missoula-based nonprofit group Cold Mountain, Cold Rivers (CMCR) had been videotaping on the Yellowstone boundary in an effort to raise awareness of the slaughter. These activists were providing footage to media outlets and concerned citizens across the country. Their footage was prominently featured on national network news reports. During the winter of 1996–97, the group sent footage of the carnage to members of the Lakota tribe in South Dakota. These were the first images Rosalie saw of the Yellowstone slaughter. Outraged, she and Arvol Looking Horse organized the Gardiner prayer.

After her arrest, Rosalie met Mike Mease, a CMCR videographer whose life had been changed by scenes he was filming. Wanting to do more than stand on the sidelines and film the killing, he shared some ideas with Rosalie. Together they decided to start a front-line organization based on public education, media exposure, political pressure, and civil disobedience—one that would shine a constant spotlight on the actions of the DOL. Rosalie, lending the group the Lakota term that expresses her peoples' relationship with the buffalo, called the group Buffalo Nations.

The campaign came together in spring 1997. I volunteered in December. Spending all of my days with the buffalo, I began to learn. To experience community, sit and watch a herd for a morning. On patrol one day, I watched as an old bull, injured in a fence during a DOL hazing operation, ducked off of the trail and collapsed. Before the agents could reach him, six more bulls, burrowing their noses under his body, lifted him to his feet and supported him as he walked to the safety of some nearby willows where the DOL's snowmobiles couldn't penetrate.

I began to watch the buffalo more carefully, observing for the first time the way a herd travels through snow in single file, taking shifts at breaking trail and sharing in the work. Living in a cabin and working with dozens of activists has its parallels with the family-oriented lives of bison. Like the injured bull and his kin, we had to watch out for one another through very difficult times and the harshest of weather. A buffalo herd, to defend itself against predators like wolves, forms an outward-facing circle. The perimeter is composed of the strongest bulls and cows—a living fortress of strength and horns to protect the old, the young, the weak, and the injured. Buffalo know how to take care of one another.

Watching these animals and incorporating their lessons into our lives adds a dimension to patrols. Decisions are made easier with experience from our time in the presence of buffalo. Asking, "What would the old bull at Duck Creek do in this situation?" yields surprising insight, at once reminding us why we are here and providing new perspective on our lives. Integrating buffalo lessons into our human community strengthens the connections between us and makes us more effective as buffalo protectors.

Not that we don't make mistakes. During our first winter in the field, developing strategy as we went along, we made plenty of them. When the killing started in January 1998, the DOL caught us by surprise. We always try to have at least one person on every morning patrol who had been on afternoon patrol in the same place on the previous day. This person, knowing exactly where the bison were last seen, can find them quickly in the dawn. On the morning of January 29, 1998, we were unprepared. No one on the morning patrol had been out the day before, and they couldn't find the six buffalo that we'd been watching for more than a month. At sunrise, Corey Mascio, a seventeen-year-old volunteer, searched:

> *I was heading down the trail at sunrise when I passed the DOL. The guns on their backs were for the buffalo. I turned to follow them. Suddenly they made a sharp left and stopped; they had found them. I pulled my sled between the guns and the buffalo. I knew that's what I'd do. There was no soul searching, none of that. It is why I'm here. The cops cuffed me. The DOL agents shot all six buffalo while I sat there watching, helpless. I fell to my knees and cried, and screamed, and prayed. That was the hardest, the darkest, most frustrating thing I have ever witnessed or been a part of. Rosalie helped me understand that my pain and my grief made me stronger. At first I couldn't understand it, but now I know I was there for a reason and I am all the stronger for it.*

The day shattered the illusion that we could prevent the DOL from killing buffalo. Three cows and three calves were dead; their blood stained the snow at Horse Butte. We slouched in our chairs through dinner. Some people argued and accused at the meeting, while others cried, forever changed by the day's events. We discussed our mistakes and adjusted for the next day's shifts. Buffalo, we realized, would continue to die. No matter how many of us there are at any given time, the government can arrest and remove us, as they did with Corey, and shoot the bison. We had prevented the killing until that day. Corey's incarceration and the ensuing gunshots redefined the way we thought of our work.

After dinner, Rosalie recommended that we go outside as a group and form a circle. She said the spiritual nature of our work and the shame and guilt we were feeling at having "allowed" six buffalo to be killed warranted a circle of prayer. Some volunteers were uneasy with the idea of an organized prayer circle. Rosalie's suggestion and her offer to lead the prayer were greeted with downcast eyes and silence. In the end, though, even those who had initially been opposed to the idea came outside and joined hands.

Although the sun had sunk behind the Madison Range, its light—the soft and subtle hues just before darkness—illuminated the snowy world around us. I'll never forget the way it all looked just then: the snow-laden branches of the Douglas firs on the hill behind the cabin, the expanse of clear sky over Hebgen Lake, Rodeo's tipi with its spiral of smoke frozen above, and the faces in the circle.

When we were all gathered and holding hands, Rosalie broke the silence:

> *Were it not for the gifts of food, clothing, and shelter provided by the Buffalo, our People would have died of starvation. We have followed the Buffalo, protected the Buffalo, lived among the Buffalo, and depended on the Buffalo for centuries. All of us gathered in this circle, and those who are with us in thought and prayer, are part of our prophecies, which tell of the return of the Buffalo Nation.*

We took turns speaking from our hearts around the circle. Everyone was asked to say a prayer.

"Tunkashala, thank you for calling us together around the buffalo. We come from different places and lead different lives. Let us be as one in our efforts to help the buffalo."

"May we be more effective next time in protecting the buffalo. Let them one day walk where they choose without being harassed for crossing meaningless lines that they cannot see."

"Help us forgive the men who pull the trigger out of ignorance, sending the buffalo to their needless deaths. Forgive the one we met in the snow who taunted us with his proud boasts of having killed so many."

"Please help us share the buffalo's story with the world, with clear and strong voices. Give us the courage to face the trials of many winters and the strength to stand beside the buffalo until they are free."

After each of us had spoken, we dropped our hands and formed smaller, spontaneous circles. Some of us were in tears, while others smiled freely. We hugged and chatted, feeling better; connected, renewed, and ready—as ready as one can be—for the coming winter. That first prayer circle helped more than any of us could have imagined. Not only did it ease our feelings of grief and powerlessness, it helped us connect with the buffalo in a more meaningful way. To many of us, middle-class white kids reared in the materialism of our culture, the prayer ceremony was an introduction to a different possibility. It helped us feel the connections between our lives, the lives of other species, and the earth beneath our feet.

As winter progressed and we became more confident of our group identity and responsibilities, we began to see less and less of Rosalie. Assured that the group was strong enough to continue without her, she left to focus her energy on organizing tribal support for the buffalo and quickly found herself embroiled in an administrative tangle.

A host of bureaucratic agencies, including the National Park Service, the US Forest Service, APHIS, the Montana DOL, and the Montana FWP, were in the process of writing a draft environmental impact statement (EIS) on bison management without consulting the people who knew the buffalo best: the tribes. Rosalie committed herself to making the tribal voice heard and demanding that Native Americans be given an active role in all management decisions affecting the herd.

Because Rosalie was no longer directly involved in our work, and because the name Buffalo Nations holds such powerful meaning to the Lakota, we consented to change the name of our group. We knew that, whatever we called ourselves, our primary focus—defending the buffalo—would remain unchanged. Since then, we've been known as Buffalo Field Campaign, but our mission—to defend the buffalo in their traditional habitat and to advocate for their protection—remains the same.

Rosalie continues to advocate for Native American representation in matters affecting the buffalo. Asserting federal law and the language from treaties, Rosalie has been pressing for increased tribal involvement. An executive order signed by President Clinton in May 1998 guaranteed the rights of tribal governments to representation in decisions affecting their communities:

> *Each agency shall have an effective process to permit elected officials and other representatives of Indian tribal governments to provide meaningful and timely input in the development of regulatory policies on matters that significantly or uniquely affect their communities.*

Does the Yellowstone buffalo herd, the last vestige of the wild millions that once roamed the plains, "significantly and uniquely" affect the Native American community?

Why, then, weren't the tribes given the opportunity to "provide meaningful and timely input" into the creation of the buffalo-management plan? Why didn't the government officials charged with buffalo management want them there? The fact that tribes weren't consulted until the last year of the eight-year process to write the EIS infuriates many of the tribal representatives who commented on the project. To James Garrett of the Cheyenne River Lakota Nation, the National Park Service's actions are a slap in the face. They are "mixing consultation with insultation. Being consulted at the eleventh hour is tantamount to insult," he said. Fred Dubray, also of the Cheyenne River Reservation, concurs:

> *For the last eight years, our tribal people have been trying to participate in this process, but we've been constantly told this [bison-management plan] has no impact on Indian people. "We only include the people that are being impacted," which is APHIS, the US Forest Service, the state of Montana, and the National Park Service. We asked for a place, a seat at that table to have a tribal representative there, and we've been consistently told there's no impact.*

The fact that no contemporary Indian reservations are contiguous with Yellowstone's borders allows government officials to ignore the spiritual and physical connections between the buffalo and the Buffalo Nations.

Having been denied access to official management decisions, the tribes sought to influence the proposal through the submission of public comments. The bison EIS generated more comments from the Native American community than any other EIS in history. Comments submitted by sovereign tribes, nongovernmental organizations, and concerned citizens were given equal weight. A letter submitted by the National Congress of American Indians—an organization representing 315 tribes—was counted the same as a single comment submitted by an individual.

Tribal representation is shunned by so-called "land managers," who feel threatened by the presence, knowledge, understanding, and spiritual engagement of the tribes who know the buffalo best. The tribes are excluded because the power of their relationship with the buffalo undermines the hegemony of the official managers. "The buffalo and the Lakota," Rosalie says, "share a common history and an inseparable destiny." Until the dignity and sovereignty of America's original human inhabitants are respected, the slaughter and domestication of Yellowstone buffalo will continue.

In the end, the draft EIS—which outlined seven possible alternatives for bison management—didn't contain a single option that would stop the slaughter of Yellowstone buffalo. Rosalie considers the process redundant, likening it to the question, "Which way do you want us to kill the buffalo?"

To slaughter buffalo without consulting the people who know them best runs counter to common sense. The slaughter is a physical affront to the Plains tribes, whose concerns fall on deaf ears while the stockman's influence is felt on all levels of government. To the livestock industry, cattle represent an economic interest and way of life that are barely a hundred years old. To the Plains tribes, buffalo represent the essence of a social, cultural, and spiritual identity going back at least 10,000 years. The tribes have been kept away from the table while the land managers, politicians, and ranchers dictate the fate of the Yellowstone buffalo.

Nineteenth-century officials condoned the slaughter of millions of buffalo because they knew it would destroy the Indians' independence. Today's leaders are doing much the same. Because of their unique relationship with the buffalo, because they are legally considered sovereign nations, and because matters affecting the buffalo affect their communities, the Plains nations should have had representation on the team that drafted the management plan. The Yellowstone ecosystem is the last refuge for the last population of wild buffalo in America. Where else can the Plains tribes engage in their ancient spiritual and physical relationship with buffalo if not in and around Yellowstone?

four

Cattle and Control: A History of Western Violence

The past is never dead. It is not even past.

—William Faulkner

I VIDEOTAPE THE OPERATION FROM THE UPPER LIMBS OF A LODGEPOLE pine on the park side of the property owner's fence. Five buffalo—a bull, a cow, and three calves—are in the trap. The bull and the cow are locked in two pens, and the three calves share another. A DOL agent rides a bobcat tractor into the first pen and lunges at the bull, pushing him toward the long corridor on the far side of the pen. The bull runs from the machine through the open doorway and down the chute toward the back of the trap. A different agent reaches over the wall from his perch on a platform and prods the buffalo with a long stick as the tractor backs off. He pounds on the bull with the cattle prod, shouting "CHAO! CHAO!" as he jerks the animal through the trap. Each touch of the prod ignites an explosion of horn or hoof against steel.

The bull has nowhere to go. At the end of the narrowing chute, he is confined by his desire to be free. The harder he pushes, the tighter his body is wedged. A steel door slams closed behind him, cutting off all chance of retreat. Pressed by hard steel from all sides, he moves the only way he can— up—and slams his head against a metal grate. Other agents work the controls of a stockade-like clamp that closes around the buffalo's neck from each side, and 2,000 pounds of pure wildness heave and thrust against the trap's jaws. The arm of one of the agents emerges from a small opening in the wall and plunges a needle into the buffalo's flesh. The bull is strong and determined, bucking and kicking until the tranquilizer hits his brain. After his final twitch, the agents smile and congratulate one another, triumphant in their mastery over the bull's wild strength.

I've witnessed scenes like these more times than I care to remember. The agents' mistreatment of the bison sparks in me the urge to run out and interfere or to hurl hurtful words across the space between us. But my work requires control. No matter how hot the flare of anger, how deep the sadness, or how infuriating the frustration, I try to hold my composure. If we act out of spite or insult, the agents will only make it harder on the buffalo and erode our efforts to gain public support for their protection. Knowing this intellectually is one thing. Holding my tongue as I watch gloating men malign buffalo is another.

Winters with the buffalo provide a lesson in extremes. Peaceful days of basking in Yellowstone's winter beauty suddenly dissolve into fierce and ugly violence. When my patience is all but spent, the only hope of refuge is to remember days when the DOL agents are not around. I conjure quiet mornings and picture myself as calm and unconcerned with revenge as the buffalo are, whose silhouettes in the sunrise resemble mountains against the sky. Quiet hours in their presence provide the balance to withstand disconcerting gun blasts, incessantly whining snowmobiles, and the all-pervading pounding of helicopter rotors. Without the calm days with buffalo, I would crack under the strain of watching the destruction of one of the last remnants of true wildness left in the world.

The ancestors of today's Yellowstone bison once ranged from the eastern seaboard to Oregon and from northern Mexico and Florida to Great Slave Lake in northern Canada. The heart of their habitat was the American Great Plains, a grassland ecosystem extending from the Rocky Mountains east to the hundredth meridian and running from northern Alberta in Canada to southern Texas. Although no one will ever know exactly how many bison once inhabited North America, recent scientific estimates put the figure between twenty-five and thirty million animals. In terms of biomass, North America's bison comprised the largest concentration of animals known to exist. According to William Hornaday, a nineteenth-century naturalist with a deep interest in bison:

> *It would have been as easy to count or to estimate the number of leaves in a forest as to calculate the number of buffaloes living at any given time during the history of the species previous to 1870.*

The nineteenth-century eradication of inestimable numbers of American buffalo is a story familiar to anyone who has taken a high-school history course. Most people, however, received an oversimplified version of events. History books often portray the near-extinction as the sole result of a US government policy to eradicate the buffalo and thereby defeat the Indian tribes who depended upon them for survival. While it may be true that the government pursued such a policy, the disappearance of tens of millions of buffalo from the Great Plains was the result of a convergence of many forces. Central among them was the growth of the Euro-American market economy and the emergence of the livestock industry in the West.

The bison's first brush with the market economy came in the form of the fur trade. A scarcity in beaver pelts, brought on by hundreds of years of market-driven trapping, shifted the burden of the fur trade to bison. By the end of the 1850s, millions of bison were being killed annually to satisfy the demand for their robes, and their numbers began to fall. According to F. F. Gerard, a Cree interpreter and trader who was employed with the American Fur Company in the mid-nineteenth century, nearly a million and a half buffalo were killed for their robes in the upper Missouri region in 1857 alone.

Romantic tales of buffalo hunts in the West increased the popularity of recreational hunts. Easterners and Europeans pined for robes of their own— as much for their romantic value as for their superior warmth. Grown to keep bison alive through some of North America's most severe winters, buffalo robes provided unparalleled warmth. They were the material of choice for covers on sleighs, wagons, and coaches and were used as blankets and tailored into winter coats.

The railroads connected the West with East Coast markets and played a watershed role in the bison's brush with extinction. Buffalo steaks provided a cheap and abundant food source for railroad workers. Companies hired hunters to shoot buffalo as food for their track-laying crews, instantly creating a new incentive to kill bison. William "Buffalo Bill" Cody earned his name and fame as a contractor with the Kansas Pacific Railroad as a buffalo hunter. He excelled in this line of work and bragged of killing 4,280 buffalo in an eighteen-month period.

While demand for buffalo robes and meat undoubtedly took a heavy toll on the bison, demand for their hides pushed them to the brink of extinction. The 1871 development of a means to convert raw hides into leather sealed the buffalos' fate. This industrial process revolutionized the buffalo hunter's work, removing the temporal limitations of hand tanning and making it possible to sell as many hides as the hunter could shoot and skin. Hides could be stored and shipped raw as soon as they dried in the sun. Millions of buffalo were gunned down for the skin on their backs, their carcasses discarded and left to rot where they'd fallen.

East Coast mills rendered hides into armor, book bindings, and shock-absorbing springs for carts and wagons. Bison hides, unparalleled in strength and elasticity, were the material of choice for the drive belts on the presses and machines powering the Industrial Revolution. Responding to the new demand, "buffalo runners"—as the hide hunters romantically called themselves—flocked to the plains.

Suddenly bound to the global economy, the buffalo were doomed. Where steamships had previously enabled tanned robes to be shipped, railroads made it possible to send vast quantities of untanned hides to the East Coast. Trains brought thousands of hunters to the plains and hauled millions of hides away.

Railroad advertising campaigns increased demand for robes in eastern markets and planted daydreams of adventure in the minds of well-to-do adventure seekers and sportsmen from the East and from Europe. It became fashionable and patriotic for train passengers to blast buffalo from the roofs and windows of moving cars. One firsthand account describes a church-sponsored hunting expedition in which passengers assembled into a cornet band to play "Yankee Doodle" over the corpse of a bull buffalo they'd just gunned down.

The railroads cut an industrial swath across the buffalos' central range, physically dividing the plains. Increased hunting and human activity along the train corridors split the herd into northern and southern sub-herds. Both were quickly diminished and all but extinguished. By 1880, the entire southern herd and all but a vestige of the northern herd were gone. The bison's demise ended the migratory ways of the horse-mounted Indian tribes and cleared the way for the rapid rise of livestock as a powerful industry in the West.

The presence of the livestock industry has had a profound impact on the buffalo and the plains ever since. One contemporary scholar describes the industry's initial impact on the buffalo:

> There were probably no more than 3 or 4 million cattle in the West, mostly in Texas, in 1865 when the war ended. Two decades later, the figure was 26 million, along with nearly 20 million sheep. The diminished range resource, coupled with excessive hunting, drove out the buffalo, the main competitor for forage.

The railroads made it possible to raise cattle in the rural West and sell them in eastern markets. Before railroads arrived in the West, Texas had produced more livestock than any western state. Ranchers had built a local economy around the longhorn—a lithe breed of Spanish cattle gone semi-wild in the Southwest. Early Texas missions maintained longhorn herds, and cattle escapees populated the Texas grasslands. Some were rounded up and domesticated and others were hunted for meat, but prior to the Civil War, there was very little demand for Texas cattle outside the state.

The post–Civil War economic boom created a new cattle economy in the West and stimulated the demand for beef. The growing middle and upper classes had a nearly insatiable appetite for beef, and the postwar economic boom gave them the purchasing power to appease it. With railroads reaching farther and farther west, ranchers began shipping livestock to eastern markets.

Millions of cattle, sometimes in herds exceeding 10,000, were driven north from Texas to the railroad depots. Between 1866 and 1884, more than five million cattle were driven north from Texas. Feedlots sprang up around the railroad stations as more and more ranchers discovered that their herds could be sustained on the northern range. In the coming years, thousands of cattle were put to pasture on the public domain, devouring prime bison habitat. An article in an 1867 Kansas newspaper described the scene:

> The entire country, east, west, and south of Salina down to the Arkansas River and Wichita, is now filled with Texas cattle. There are not only cattle on a thousand hills but a thousand cattle on one hill and every hill. The bottoms are overflowing with them and the water courses with this great article of traffic. Perhaps not less than 200,000 of them are in the state, 60,000 of which are within a day's ride of Salina, and the cry is, "Still they come."

It is no coincidence that the 1870s, the bloodiest decade for the buffalo, saw an exponential rise in the number of cattle on the plains. Even without the slaughter, bison populations would have been hard-hit by the increasing numbers of cattle. The newly introduced ungulates infected bison with European diseases to which they had no previous exposure or immunity and degraded the grasslands on which they fed. Between 1874 and 1880, cattle numbers in Wyoming jumped from 90,000 to more than 500,000. By 1883, eastern Montana was also home to more than half a million cattle, which soon replaced buffalo as the dominant plains grazer. In the words of Richard Dodge, a firsthand observer: "For every single buffalo that roamed the plains in 1871, there are in 1881 not less than two, and more probably four or five, of the descendants of the long-horned cattle of Texas. The destroyers of the buffalo are followed by the preservers of the cattle."

During the 1870s, more buffalo were shot than in any other decade in history. The three years from 1872 through 1874 were the worst. According to one buffalo runner, who based his estimate on firsthand accounts and shipping records, at least four and a half million buffalo were slaughtered in the three years between 1872 and 1874. By the end of the 1870s, the buffalo were nearly gone. A chapter in history, tens of thousands of years in the unfolding, came to a sudden end.

Eradicating the buffalo helped to conquer the Indians and generated demand for beef in the process. Tribes that had been self-sufficient for millennia were suddenly forced to subsist on government rations. Ironically, these handouts consisted largely of beef. In 1880, the US government brought 39,160,729 pounds of beef from western ranches "to be delivered on the hoof at 34 Indian Agencies in ten western states." To the early western livestock industry, these government contracts were a major boon.

Granville Stuart, a pioneering Montana rancher who profited from the bison's demise, described the wasteful bloodshed in 1880:

> The bottoms are literally sprinkled with the carcasses of dead buffalo. In many places, they lie thick on the ground, fat and meat not yet spoiled, all murdered for their hides which are piled like cordwood all along the way. . . . Probably ten thousand buffalo have been killed in this vicinity this winter (1879–1880).

General Nelson Miles predicted the rise of the livestock industry in 1876: "When we get rid of the Indians and buffalo, the cattle will fill this country." Francis Parkman saw it coming even earlier. In his preface to the 1872 edition of *The Oregon Trail*, he wrote:

> A time would come when those plains would be a grazing country, the buffalo give place to tame cattle, farmhouses be scattered along the watercourses, and wolves, bears, and Indians be numbered among the things that were.

Parkman was right. Cattle soon filled the buffalos' niche on the plains. A remnant bison herd avoided the fate of its kin by holing up in the Pelican Valley, in the Yellowstone interior. The descendants of this herd continue to travel between the Pelican Valley and other areas within and around Yellowstone. They are the bison with which I spend my winters—the ones I watch being shot and trapped each winter.

From my perch in the tree on the park boundary, I videotape as DOL agents push and prod five of these buffalo through the trap. They now have the female in the squeeze chute. Like the bull before her, she pushes and pulls against the clamped steel jaws. The panels of the trap rattle in their hinges, splintering the still morning air. After one very loud crash, the agent controlling the squeeze chute smiles and shouts, "She's a live one, ain't she?"

I hear a voice cry out, "Not for long, thanks to you!" and realize it is mine. The agents working the trap don't look up. Two Montana highway patrolmen walk out from behind the facility, scanning the trees through binoculars.

They come over and stand at the base of my tree. One of them says to the other, "Say, Jim, have you seen those tree huggers lately?"

Jim answers, "No, but I smell 'em."

"Hey, tree huggers," the first patrolman calls. "Why don't you come down and start looking for a job?" They both chuckle.

Such conversations are doomed from the start, and this one is no different. I shout down, "I'd rather hug a tree than you," then realize how petty it sounds.

Jim laughs and says, "That's not what your mother says."

I almost tell him, my mother's dead, you asshole, but bite my tongue instead, wishing I had kept my mouth shut from the start.

The sound of steel on steel sends chills through my bones as the trap groans in protest of its task. The buffalo is quaking now, out of place and distressed in the steel maze. Watching her tremble in the cage, I try to imagine how the squeeze chute must feel to a creature honed over centuries for life on the fenceless plains.

I stare down on the scene through the camera lens and pan to the police car on the far side of the trap. Painted on its door are the Montana Highway Patrol insignia and the numbers "3-7-77." The same cryptic insignia is emblazoned on the shoulder patches of the heckling officers. The numbers are a reference to Montana's early vigilantes, who etched the symbol as a warning onto the front doors of those whom they did not like. Vigilantism was prevalent among Montana's early mining camps and later among ranchers. Granville Stuart, an early and influential rancher, was known to have organized vigilance committees.

To this day, no one knows the meaning behind the mysterious numbers 3-7-77. Some think that they signify the dimensions of a grave: three feet wide, seven feet long, and seventy-seven inches deep. Others say that the numbers represent a period of time—three hours, seven minutes, and seventy-seven seconds—that the vigilantes gave potential victims to flee before killing them. Others, failing to account for the final pair of sevens, insist that they were a reference to the three-dollar fare on the 7 A.M. train from Helena to Butte. Whatever their meaning, the message was clear: Leave town or we'll take your life.

Watching the officers on the ground, I wonder if they ever consider the significance of the numbers on their shoulder patches and police-car doors. I look down at the policemen standing beside the cattle detectives and consider the long relationship between Montana cattlemen and the law.

The buffalo caged below is only the latest example in a cycle of violence originating with the western livestock industry. DOL employees assigned to the buffalo slaughter were given the power to arrest in 1998. Many of my friends and fellow workers have been arrested or detained by DOL agents. The agency responsible for protecting and promoting Montana's livestock industry is now entrusted to incarcerate citizens for alleged violation of laws having nothing to do with livestock.

Enforcement of general laws is a role long coveted by livestock producers. Granville Stuart, first president of the Board of Stock Commissioners (a precursor to the DOL), wrote of the importance of giving stock inspectors the power to make arrests for crimes unrelated to livestock in 1887:

> *The Stock Detectives have rendered material aid in the enforcement of the law and the capture and conviction of offenders, not only against the stock interests of Montana, but in the general enforcement of its criminal laws.*

The wealthy ranchers who hired the stock detectives did not take kindly to small-scale homesteaders, who threatened their exclusive control of the land and their way of life. Under the General Homestead Act of 1862—designed to encourage settlement of the West by small, family farmers—settlers could earn title to 160 acres if they could prove, over time, their ability to earn a living from it. These struggling homesteaders quickly found themselves victims of an undeclared war.

Cattle producers were vehemently opposed to homesteading, which broke their stranglehold on vast expanses of public land, excluded cattle from some of the most fertile and well-watered areas, and spelled an end to their monopoly of the West. To protect themselves against the homesteaders, the ranchers made fraudulent claims under the Homestead Act and illegally secured the surrounding lands. Recruiting strangers and hiring ranch hands to make claims was a preferred method of maintaining control over their public-land empires. When this became impracticable, the ranchers resorted to more nefarious tactics.

The industry has a long history of lethally eradicating human and animal competitors in its crusade for control of the public domain. Cattle barons, accustomed to controlling vast expanses of public land, were threatened by the wave of homesteaders settling the West in the last decades of the nineteenth century. Understanding that the new homesteads would break their hegemonic hold on the landscape, the ranchers used their power to intimidate the competition. Many settlers were accused of rustling the ranchers' stock. Many were killed without ever being formally charged, tried, convicted, or sentenced.

The tensions between homesteaders and ranchers were exacerbated in the wake of the winter of 1886–87, when thousands of range cattle across the plains starved to death during a winter of extreme cold and heavy snows. The "Big Die Up," as the winter has come to be called, put many of the early cattle barons out of business. The few who survived the ordeal with the will to continue ranching resolved to defend their industry against any threats over which they could exert any level of control. The growing waves of settlers became targets of the cattle barons and livestock associations.

Homesteaders were shot, hanged, burned to death, or—if they were lucky—banished. In northern Wyoming, a succession of such murders took place between 1889 and 1892. In July 1889, a couple was lynched after filing for a homestead on land controlled by a wealthy rancher. Two years later, three other settlers who had been openly critical of ranchers' tactics were murdered in a campaign organized by stock growers.

The violence culminated in the Johnson County Invasion of April 1892, when the leaders of the Wyoming Stock Growers Association hired a militia to invade northern Wyoming and assassinate dozens of people on a list compiled by wealthy ranchers. The association sought to make an example of the settlers and reverse the influx of settlers moving into northern Wyoming.

The Stock Growers Association was the most powerful political organization in Wyoming at the time, with influence on Wyoming's governor and attorney general, a judge, both US senators, and the president of the United States. Gunmen were hired on a five-dollar per diem, given guns from the state arsenal, and offered fifty dollars for each confirmed kill. More than $100,000 was spent on the invasion. The invaders carried a list with the names of seventy settlers and officials whom the association wanted dead. Among the names were Buffalo's sheriff and mayor, the county commissioners, businessmen, a newspaper editor, and assorted settlers.

The invading army was comprised of fifty-two men, including nine members of the Executive Committee of the Wyoming Stock Growers Association, deputy US marshals, wealthy ranchers and managers, and

twenty-two Texas mercenaries. Rumors of the invasion, which had been cir-
culating northern Wyoming for months, were confirmed on April 5 when
an unusual six-car train was seen heading north from Cheyenne. The special train—including a Pullman car with blinds drawn, three cars full of
horses, a flatcar carrying three Studebaker wagons, and a car for baggage,
munitions, and equipment—was an unusual sight in the Cheyenne yards.

The invaders' first stop was the cabin of two supposed rustlers, whom
they surrounded in the night. One of the men was shot when he came out for
water in the morning. The other, a skilled marksman named Nate Champion, held off the attackers for the better part of the day and even found time
to write in his journal as he did so. Here are his final words, written moments
before he bolted through a window to his death:

> Well, they have just got through shelling the house like hail. I heard
> them splitting wood. I guess they are going to fire the house to-night.
> I think I will make a break when night comes, if alive. Shooting again.
> I think they will fire the house this time. It's not night yet. The house is
> all fire. Good-bye, boys, if I never see you again.

Having accomplished the first two deaths on a list of seventy, the Stock
Growers' army made way for Buffalo, where they planned to blow up the
courthouse and shoot settlers as they tried to flee. Fortunately, word of the
attack had already reached the city, and 200 angry citizens had quickly organized to defend themselves. The invaders, learning of this resistance,
retreated and holed up in a fortified ranch. The angry townspeople surrounded them and held them captive for two days until the US Cavalry
arrived and the invaders surrendered. Although they were detained for a
short time, the political influence of the Stock Growers Association ensured
that none of the invaders was sentenced to jail.

Montana's ranching pioneers employed similar tactics. Granville Stuart
organized a vigilance committee known as Stuart's Stranglers to lynch a
gang of suspected horse thieves. Stuart's vigilantes set fire to a cabin full of
sleeping suspects early one July morning in 1884. Five people burned to

death in the blaze. The four who managed to escape were later hunted down by the aptly named Stranglers and were promptly lynched. Before the killing spree was over, at least nineteen accused rustlers and the men who were unfortunate enough to be in their presence were killed. According to a contemporary of Stuart, such killing of innocent bystanders was common at the time: "You run with horse thieves, them days, you hung with them."

Such attacks were not isolated instances of individual cowboys seeking revenge on people who had spited them. They were organized attempts on the part of the prominent stock growers to maintain power and control. While all ranchers didn't participate in or even support such tactics, they were embraced by the livestock associations and overwhelmingly supported by the most powerful ranchers. One rancher, who lived in the area where the arson took place, said it was not carried out "by bands of lawless cowboys but was the result of a general understanding among all the large cattle ranges of Montana." Granville Stuart was named president of the newly formed Montana Stock Growers Association that same year.

Homesteaders and "rustlers" were not the only victims. Fifty-three thousand sheep and dozens of sheepmen were slaughtered by western cattle ranchers between 1880 and 1920 in a series of bloody conflicts known as the Cattle/Sheep Wars. Cattlemen, unwilling to share the public-range resource with sheepmen, resorted to violence to preserve the status quo. Sheepmen refusing the ranchers' warnings faced death threats and the prospect of having their flocks slaughtered. Sheepmen and shepherds were sometimes kidnapped, beat up, or killed while their flocks were shot, clubbed to death, or stampeded over cliffs. This technique of "rim rocking," as the ranchers called it, was adapted from the buffalo jumps of the Plains Indians.

The Bear Creek Raid of December 27, 1900, provides a good example of a rancher's typical response to the increasing number of sheep on the public domain. Northern Wyoming cattle rancher John Kendrick, who illegally laid claim to the valleys east of the Big Horn Mountains in Wyoming and Montana, was infuriated when Robert Selway, a sheepman, brought his flocks onto the public lands of southeastern Montana. Kendrick and his neighbor, George Brewster, organized a posse of local cowboys to carry out the dirty work. Riding to the sheep camp before dawn, the eleven men in the cattlemen's posse held the lone shepherd at gunpoint and proceeded to club the defenseless sheep to death. Before sunset, the cowboys had slaughtered the entire herd of 3,000 animals without firing a single shot.

The sheriff, himself a cattle rancher, found the bloody clubs but refused to investigate or prosecute anyone in the case. Instead, he mockingly assured Selway that he would arrest the first person that came in to claim one of the clubs. Although they were never charged, Kendrick and Brewster enjoyed a bit of local notoriety for their parts in the raid. Brewster used the resulting popularity to gain election to the Montana House of Representatives in 1905, 1907, and 1909 and to the presidency of the Montana Stock Growers Association in 1911. Kendrick would go on to serve as president of the National Livestock Association, governor of Wyoming, and US senator.

This violent chain of events didn't die with the persecuted homesteaders or the slaughtered sheep. The livestock industry's use of intimidation and slaughter to eliminate predators and competitors has continued to the present day. The nineteenth-century cattle-baron-sponsored killing of homesteaders and sheep has its modern counterpart in the killing of coyotes, wolves, lions, bears, wild horses, prairie dogs, and bison. Understanding this uninterrupted history of violence is essential to understanding the present buffalo slaughter—the latest manifestation of the livestock industry's campaign to destroy perceived threats to its hold on the West.

Since the early days of the western territories, the industry has used its political clout to force the killing of predators. Western counties, largely controlled by stockmen, offered bounties on wild species that the ranchers wanted killed. Wolves, coyotes, and mountain lions were early targets. Montana paid bounties on 81,000 wolves between 1883 and 1918. In 1915, Congress appropriated $125,000 to the Department of Agriculture's Biological Survey for predator control. The agency used the money to hire 300 men to kill predators on public and private lands. From the ranchers' point of view, the program, which resulted in the near eradication of wolves from the western landscape, has been a success. For the rest of the American public and for the wild species themselves, the program is a travesty. The establishment of a government-sponsored predator-control program set a precedent that, as one observer put it, "opened the door to using public funds to kill publicly owned animals on public lands for the economic gain of private stockmen."

Once opened, the door would never close. The Animal Damage Control Act of 1931 created the division of Animal Damage Control (ADC) and expanded the list of animals targeted for control. Bobcats, lions, prairie dogs, and other species "injurious to agriculture and animal husbandry" joined coyotes and wolves as prime targets of government-funded killers. The expanded list, no longer limited to predators, was the result of pressure from the ranching lobby.

In 1940, the "coyote getter," a contraption designed to eject a deadly cloud of sodium cyanide into the mouth of the hungry animal attracted to the trap's scented wick, came into popular use. By the end of the decade, an arsenal of dangerous chemicals had been deployed to indiscriminately poison wildlife across the West. Chief among them was compound 1080 (sodium monofluoroacetate), a poison that causes failure in the immune and cardiovascular systems of mammals and birds. These and other chemicals were mixed with meat, tallow, feed pellets, and grain and scattered across the landscape. Between 1961 and 1970, more than seven million pieces of poisoned meat and tallow and nearly a million and a half pounds of poisoned grain were dropped from airplanes, trucks, and horses by ADC agents and cooperating agencies.

Due to the indiscriminate nature of poison bait and traps—and the vast expanses across which they were spread—approximate numbers of targeted and non-targeted species killed are impossible to ascertain. But numbers of confirmed kills in the seventeen western states give an idea of the slaughter's magnitude. According to its own figures, the ADC killed more than 809,000 animals in 1990, including 91,158 coyotes; 8,144 skunks; 9,363 beavers; 7,065 foxes; 5,933 raccoons; 1,083 porcupines; and 3,463 opossums.

One firsthand account, from a former ADC agent, paints a vivid picture of the magnitude of the slaughter on a local scale and of the attitudes of the ranchers behind it:

*I killed so many coyotes I got ashamed of myself. I think I got 700
and some coyotes in three months. Of course next spring, I didn't notice
any difference in the amount of telephone calls I got. It was the same old
whine, "The coyotes are putting us out of business, the coyotes are eating
us up."*

Ranchers were seeing just as many coyotes because there were just as
many; the killing was compensated by an increase in birthrates. Coyote
packs are biologically wired to produce more offspring in the wake of trau-
matic events resulting in attrition.

The western livestock industry's long history of violence against competition is rooted in the fact that European cattle, demanding large quantities
of water and food throughout the year, are not suited to survival in the arid
western United States. Without taxpayer-funded subsidies like predator control, drought and fire relief, fencing, and below-cost grazing allotments,
public-lands ranching would be, at best, a money-losing pursuit. The indus-
try-organized killing of homesteaders, sheep, wolves, and bison are all
industry attempts to create ideal conditions for cattle in an environment to
which they do not belong. George Wuerthner, a prominent critic of public-
lands livestock grazing, explains the ranchers' predicament:

> *By growing domestic animals that demand large quantities of
> water and forage in a place that is dry, and by favoring slow-moving,
> heavy, and relatively defenseless livestock in terrain that is rugged, vast,
> and inhabited by native predators, ranchers have actually put them-
> selves in a position of constant warfare with the land.*

This state of perpetual warfare is reflected prominently in the cowboy
ethos. Some twenty-first-century cowboys are proud of their industry's violent heritage. Bob Peebles, former manager of the Boone and Crockett Club
Ranch on Montana's Rocky Mountain Front, told a group of visiting graduate students in 2000, "We're a product of the raping era and we can thank
our lucky stars we are." Other ranchers share Peebles's enthusiasm for their

profession's violent past. In the summer of 2001, Nevada ranchers held a rally to protest the confiscation of cattle that they were grazing illegally on the public range. A prominent placard displayed at the protest made reference to the nineteenth-century lynchings of accused cattle thieves. "Rustling is still a capital offense," it read.

Still others put pages from the past to practice, using death threats and intimidation to maintain the status quo. In 1990, Don Oman, district ranger for Idaho's Sawtooth National Forest, sought to reverse ecological damage from years of overgrazing and announced a 10 percent reduction in the number of permitted cattle. Furious ranchers, acting through the Stock Growers Association, lobbied Congress and US Forest Service administrators to have Oman transferred from the district. When this failed, a millionaire rancher named Winslow Whitely reverted to death threats: "Either Oman is gone or he's going to have an accident," he said. "Myself and every other one of the permit holders would cut his throat if we could get him alone." When asked if he was making a threat on Oman's life, Whitely responded, "Yes, it's intentional. If they don't move him out of this district, we will."

The death threats against Whitely testify to the violent tendencies of an industry rigid in its resistance to change. Cattle producers, seeking to maximize profits, have been slow to read the ecological signs of overgrazing. Oman's attempt to reduce the number of cattle on grazing allotments within the Sawtooth came only after he documented firsthand the effects of too many cows: "deepening gullies, soil erosion, [and] dried-up creeks." The ranchers' push to have Oman removed—and even the death threats he received—are typical. The political clout of the range-cattle industry is strong enough to stifle reform. The resulting overgrazing continues to denude vast expanses of the western landscape, fosters the spread of exotic species, reduces biodiversity, arrests natural succession, and diminishes the biomass and density of native plants and animals.

In Montana and other western states, the cowboy myth is stronger than the reality. Old West images of cowboys herding stock across Montana's open range obscure the fact that public-lands ranching in Montana contributes less than one-quarter of 1 percent of total US beef production. Private lands in Maryland produce as much beef as Montana's BLM and US Forest Service lands combined. It takes seventy-three times the land base to raise a cow in Montana as it does in Iowa. And Montana is not an anomaly; smaller eastern states, where rainfall is more abundant, support more livestock than their famous western counterparts. A cow can live for a year on two acres in the East; the same cow would require a hundred in the West. Florida, not exactly famous for its cattle industry, produces more beef cattle than the cowboy state of Wyoming. Louisiana produces twice as many cattle as Nevada. Ranchers, struggling to make ends meet in the arid West, have long fallen to the temptation of stocking the public range with more cattle than it can sustain.

Millions of acres of publicly owned land have been overgrazed to the point where they can no longer support native flora or fauna. According to a 1991 report issued by the GAO, continued public-lands grazing "risks long-term environmental damage while not generating revenues sufficient to provide for adequate management." The report concludes with a reference to a common argument used by ranchers in defense of their profession: "according to the [ranch] operators, [an] important benefit they do receive is the ability to maintain a traditional ranching lifestyle they enjoy." Enjoyable as it may be for its practitioners, the lifestyle is not self-sufficient. Taxpayers, rather than the ranchers themselves, bear the burden of supporting the ranching way of life.

Subsidized grazing permits give ranchers control of hundreds of millions of acres of federal land for the artificially low fee of $1.35 per AUM, the amount of forage needed to sustain one cow and her calf, one horse, or five sheep or goats for a month. In the West, this amounts to a little more than 10 percent of the $11.10 average charged on private lands. Nearly 80 percent of the land under BLM and US Forest Service management is grazed. Half of our designated wilderness areas are stocked with cattle. Overall, some 307 million acres of public land in the sixteen western states are leased to ranchers at a fraction of their market value. According to a recent study conducted by Robert Nelson, professor of environmental policy at the University of Maryland's School of Public Affairs, the BLM's grazing program cost

$200 million to administer in 1993. During the same year, the program generated just $20 million in revenues. In other words, taxpayers pay ten times as much to support the grazing program through taxes as ranchers do through grazing fees.

Despite the assistance they receive in the form of subsidies, predator control, and other programs, ranchers have an uneasy relationship with the federal government. In *Centennial*, his historical novel on cattle ranching in the American West, James Michener describes the irony of the cattleman's attitude toward the federal government:

> *All he wanted from Washington was free use of public lands, high tariff on any meat coming from Australia and Argentina, the building and maintenance of public roads, the control of predators, the provision of free education, a good mail service with free delivery to the ranch gate, and a strong sheriff's department to arrest anyone who might think of intruding on the land. "I want no interference from the government," the rancher proclaimed, and he meant it.*

The financial and ecological burdens of the Yellowstone buffalo slaughter, like public-lands grazing in general, rest on the backs of all taxpayers while relatively few livestock producers reap the benefits. The Horse Butte grazing allotment, near West Yellowstone, Montana, which was vacated in 2002, is a case in point. The Horse Butte allotment supported just 142 cow–calf pairs and brought the treasury less than $800 a year. Yet the bison-management plan, developed at the urging of Montana's livestock industry, is costing taxpayers more than three million dollars a year, most of which is funded by the federal government. This doesn't account for the tremendous ecological costs of the DOL's bison haze, capture, and slaughter operations.

Since 1998, the Horse Butte Peninsula has been the epicenter of the DOL's war on Yellowstone bison. The peninsula, located just a few miles from the western edge of Yellowstone National Park, provides crucial habitat to most of the park's native species. Bison, wolves, grizzly and black bears, deer, elk, moose, golden and bald eagles, white pelicans, trumpeter swans, sandhill cranes, and great blue herons are some of the more charismatic species who make their home in the area.

DOL operations, whether they involve hazing, capturing, or shooting bison, take a heavy toll on all species. From late fall to early spring, agents patrol this sensitive habitat in search of any bison outside the park. Shooting cracker rounds (explosive charges fired from shotguns), agents tirelessly pursue, capture, and slaughter bison. Between the deafening bursts of these explosive charges and the nerve-quaking noise of their machines, the agents disturb virtually every species in the ecosystem.

Because there are three known bald-eagle nests on Horse Butte, much of the area is officially closed to human activity, as legislated under the Endangered Species Act. Livestock agents consistently ignore the closure, flying the helicopters over the restricted zones and entering on the ground. Although Buffalo Field Campaign has presented the US Forest Service with evidence of the eagle-closure violations, including video footage and signed affidavits, the agency has never issued more than a verbal warning to the DOL. As a result, citizens were forced to file a costly lawsuit in federal court.

Ranchers have been some of the most vocal foes of the Endangered Species Act since its passage in 1973. They commonly argue that the act constitutes a "taking" of property, since it can restrict the activities in which a landowner may engage. While the industry argues broadly in favor of property rights, its motives are more narrowly focused. Jerry Jones, a spokesman for the Montana Stock Growers Association, identifies the erosion of "private property rights" as "one of the major challenges to the beef industry." He and other representatives of the association identify the Endangered Species Act as a major infringement on the rights of ranchers.

The industry's respect for property rights doesn't extend beyond the ranch gate. After watching DOL agents shoot bison in their yards and neighborhoods, many landowners on the Horse Butte Peninsula refused agents permission to enter their property. The DOL's former staff attorney, in a letter to the Montana state veterinarian, advised that the department and the livestock industry should pursue lawsuits against such property owners:

> *It has come to my attention that there were individual landowners*
> *who refused our agents access to their lands. . . . For those individuals I*
> *would suggest that . . . a charge of violation of the statutes . . . might be*
> *proper. This is a civil penalty and . . . could prove extremely expensive to*
> *that person. [Additionally,] there is the possibility of a class action*
> *against those landowners by the livestock industry. I assure you that*
> *there are attorneys who would welcome that type of case so long as you*
> *understand it only takes a preponderance of the evidence and not proof*
> *beyond a reasonable doubt.*

The letter carries echoes of the industry's nineteenth-century tactics and betrays hypocrisy in the agency's attitude toward property rights. It also contains less-than-sound legal advice. The statutes cited do not, in fact, permit DOL agents to enter private property in pursuit of buffalo. While the law does provide them with the right to "enter anywhere where there may be found [disease-infected] livestock," it does not authorize agents to enter private land to manage buffalo and other wild species.

The DOL's track record attests to this difficulty in distinguishing wild buffalo from livestock. The agents who manage the Yellowstone buffalo in Montana receive no formal training in wildlife biology or management. Wild buffalo are routinely rounded up by Stetsoned cowboys, corralled in cattle pens, and slaughtered in industrial slaughterhouses designed for livestock. On the Montana side of the park border, these attitudes translate into buffalo being killed while other wild species like moose, deer, and elk—also known to carry brucellosis—are allowed to enter Montana freely.

The boundary, a straight line drawn across the landscape, is the livestock industry's line in the sand. While the nineteenth-century slaughter was driven by fears of the pre-cattle West, the current slaughter is driven by fears of a West after cattle. Knowing that buffalo would naturally reinhabit their former range outside the park if they were allowed to, the industry insists that they be killed when they cross the line and enter Montana.

The words of Representative Omar Conger, spoken on the floor of the

US House of Representatives more than 120 years ago, reflect an attitude toward bison that is still popular within the livestock industry:

> They eat the grass. They trample upon the plains upon which our settlers desire to herd their cattle and their sheep. There is no mistake about that. They range over the very pastures where the settlers keep their herds of cattle. They destroy the pasture.

Buffalo, as they were in the 1870s, are seen as an obstacle to be overcome and as an impediment to progress. They do not respect barbed wire or allow themselves to be domesticated. With the Yellowstone herd threatening to re-establish itself on public lands surrounding the park, lands officially designated as "wildlife habitat," the livestock industry has become alarmed. Conditioned to believe that grass grows on the western landscape for the sole purpose of fattening cattle, the industry considers it unacceptable and backward for buffalo to reclaim any of their former range outside the park. Buffalo are the ultimate symbol of the truly wild nature of our continent's past and the rich potential for its future. It is precisely this potential, and the fear it inspires in the livestock industry, that fuels the needless bloodshed.

five

Direct Action

It is not desirable to cultivate a respect for the law, so much as for the right. The only obligation which I have a right to assume is to do at any time what I think right. Law never made men a whit more just; and, by means of their respect for it, even the well-disposed are daily made the agents of injustice.

—Henry David Thoreau

I PRESSED MY BACK INTO THE SWAYING TRUNK AND BRACED MYSELF through the strong gusts. Charlie lay on the dirt floor of the Horse Butte trap, locked to the base of the swinging doors between the outer corral and the holding pens. The lone security guard didn't see him climb the rim of the bluff with the lockbox, slip through the horizontal bars, and secure himself to the trap. I was in a tree on the opposite end of the capture facility, doing my best to hold on through the wind and keep Charlie centered in the camera's field of vision. My brother had put his body between the buffalo and their capture, and my video footage would be his primary protection.

Charlie's decision to go in had been cemented when we received a radio call from the Madison patrol, who said that the DOL had just started hazing fourteen buffalo toward the trap. Charlie, Mike, and I—on the Horse Butte morning patrol—were surprised by the news. The operation blatantly violated the US Forest Service permit regulating DOL operations on Horse Butte. These regulations limit bison-hazing operations near the Madison River to the hours between 10 A.M. and 3 P.M., when eagles are less likely to be foraging. Although we were used to the DOL's disregard for environmental laws, this was the first time we'd seen them break this particular one.

Under different circumstances, I would have called it a beautiful morning. We had watched the sun rise above the Yellowstone Plateau, spilling pink ripples across the snowy ridges of the Gallatin Range. The brightening day lent the sky a deep violet-blue, a color I have only seen above the Rockies. A small group of buffalo mothers, yearling calves, and one bright-yellow, newborn calf grazed 200 yards to the east of the trap. I knew of another 100 or so in scattered bands along the six-mile stretch of the Madison bluffs between Horse Butte and the Yellowstone boundary. The magic of the morning was marred by my knowledge of what I was about to see. In the next few hours, I would watch county, state, and federal agents haul my brother off to jail and herd untold numbers of buffalo into the trap.

Even with the camera zoomed in tight, I could only make out the lockbox and the bottom half of Charlie's legs. He was on his stomach, arms extended beyond his head into the lockbox, which he had positioned around the vertical post supporting the massive steel door frame. Lockboxes are composed of two sixteen-inch lengths of four-inch pipe welded together at an angle to form a V. Before sneaking into the trap, Charlie had fastened chains around his wrists. After positioning the lockbox around the post, he slid his arms into its open ends. With his forearms buried up to his elbows in the pipes, he clipped the chains to a post that was welded to the apex of the lockbox. As long as the device remained intact, Charlie's arms couldn't be pried out unless he voluntarily unclipped his wrists.

"How's he doing?" Mike shouted up from the ground. I could see Charlie's lower legs, bending at the knees, moving in a steady up-and-down rhythm that reminded me of his guitar playing, sure and steady.

"He's alright," I yelled down.

In the two weeks prior to his lockdown, Charlie had witnessed the capture of fifty-four buffalo and had seen twenty-eight shipped to slaughter. He had been on the Horse Butte patrol to document the release of thirteen buffalo and told the group at our nightly meeting how one of them could barely walk and another dripped a trail of blood from a gore wound it had received while confined in the trap. He asked me if it was common for buffalo to be injured in the trap, and I showed him video footage of two buffalo that died hours after being released by the DOL. I showed him a report in which a meat inspector describes the condition of buffalo being slaughtered for the DOL: "One bull buffalo was beat up and gored so [badly] that I had to remove one right leg and both sides of ribs—also had to trim a lot."

These experiences had influenced Charlie's decision to do a lockdown. Although he had reached this decision on his own after days of careful reflection, I couldn't help feeling responsible for my seventeen-year-old brother's safety. My video camera was Charlie's only protection from abuse at the hands of the law-enforcement officers who would be called to remove and arrest him.

If Charlie was scared, he didn't show it. I was shaking. A few weeks earlier, a volunteer named Joe had locked down to the trap to disrupt a capture operation. Unlike Charlie, Joe had locked himself inside, where he couldn't be seen and his treatment couldn't be recorded. A gung-ho security guard in his twenties had discovered him near the squeeze chute and promptly greeted him with kicks to the ribs, legs, and stomach. Although Joe filed a complaint with the sheriff's office, no action was ever taken against the guard.

When a different security guard—in his fifties and walking with a pronounced limp—discovered Charlie, he didn't kick or prod him but used his cell phone instead. After calling the DOL, he paced the distance between his car and the trap several times, glancing nervously from me to my brother. I couldn't help but feel sorry for the man, hired by a private security company and contracted out to the DOL. How many hours had he spent sitting in his car, bored, imagining shifting shapes and shadows and wishing for some action? When his chance finally came, he had missed it altogether by allowing Charlie to stroll unimpeded into the trap and bring a hazing operation to a standstill. From the way the security guard slumped his shoulders and nervously shifted his gaze, I knew he must be thinking about losing his job.

When the DOL finally arrived, fresh from their abandoned capture operation, they came in force—leading a caravan of ten trucks. The convoy included a trailer full of horses, one loaded with six ATVs, one with four snowmobiles, and another carrying a generator and a cutting torch. Accompanying the agents was the usual assortment of rangers, wardens, and law-enforcement officers representing the Montana High-way Patrol; the Gallatin County Sheriff's Department; the Montana Department of Fish, Wildlife and Parks; the National Park Service, and the US Forest Service.

Two US Forest Service law-enforcement personnel got out of their trucks and immediately approached the base of my tree. Mike, who had been on the ground tending a campfire all morning, was ordered to leave the area and stand at the cattle guard, several hundred yards to the east. He was warned that he'd be arrested if he didn't comply. As he put the fire out and started walking toward the cattle guard, they ordered me out of the tree.

"I'm not coming down," I told them. "That's my brother in there, and I'm not leaving him." The officers walked over to the trap and conferred with a DOL agent.

A few minutes later, they were back at the base of the tree. "We're going to let you stay," they said. "You just have to promise that you won't disrupt the operation."

"I'm here to shoot video," I told them, "and to support my brother."

"If you come down before the operation is over, you'll be arrested. This is your warning. Understood?"

"Understood," I shouted down. They walked back to their truck, climbed in, and turned it around so that they could watch me through the windshield.

The DOL agents and the other law-enforcement officers went to work extracting Charlie. After opening the gates to the outer corral, they backed the trailer with the generator and torch to within ten feet of him. The sound of the generator drowned out their voices, and the bodies of a dozen men blocked my view as they huddled around Charlie and went to work. I'm not sure why they fired up the generator. Charlie thinks it was to unnerve him; he says that they didn't use it to cut the lockbox, opting instead for a mechanical pipe cutter. It could have been to prevent me from recording their conversation as they tried to persuade my brother into unlocking himself.

They told him they'd have to cut the trap and that he'd be responsible for thousands of dollars in damages. They told him he'd "go to jail for a long time" and that if he'd just unlock himself, his punishment would be less severe. He didn't do it. After about an hour, they had severed the lockbox, handcuffed my brother, and led him to the back of the sheriff's SUV.

"We're proud of you, Charlie!" I shouted as the deputy sheriff put him in the back of the car. As I videotaped the car disappearing down the road, I noticed that the small buffalo herd that had been standing near the trap had wandered north and was grazing inside the eagle closure. As long as they stayed in there, they'd be safe. While the early morning capture attempt had illustrated the DOL's disregard for environmental regulations, I knew that they didn't want to strengthen our legal case with another violation of the eagle closure.

In 1998 and again in 2000, we documented DOL operations that were in clear violation of the ESA. On both occasions, we videotaped as the agency flew its helicopter inside a Forest Service closure established under the ESA to protect nesting eagles on Horse Butte. The DOL was never issued more than a verbal warning for these violations, which have been taken seriously by neither the Forest Service nor the courts. In the same time period, dozens of bison advocates were arrested as they attempted to point out inconsistencies in the law and hold the agencies accountable for their part in the buffalo slaughter.

Since promising the judge that they wouldn't violate the closure again, the DOL had stuck to its word. With me in the tree and other video cameras at the cattle guard, a violation might have resulted in the revocation of the DOL's permit to haze and capture buffalo on Horse Butte.

Once Charlie was out of the way, the agents regrouped. After saddling their horses and backing their four-wheelers and snowmobiles off of the trailers, they rode away to resume their capture operation along the Madison bluffs. The two Forest Service law-enforcement officers drove over and parked by the cattle guard, where Mike and a half dozen other volunteers stood waiting. I hung the camera from a nearby branch, rested against another, closed my eyes, and took a deep breath.

I knew it would be hours before the armada of agents reappeared, hounding a herd of frightened bison, and I tried to prepare myself. The day's events marked the fifteenth killing operation of the winter. The act of witnessing capture operations doesn't get easier with experience. Watching the last wild buffalo being ripped by the hundreds from the roots of their ancestral lands and trucked to an industrial slaughterhouse is an experience I will never forget. Buffalo are such beautiful, spiritual beings; their treatment by the DOL is the most horrendous human behavior I have seen. Horrible scenes of buffalo in the trap haunt my nightmares.

Trying to clear my head of slaughter thoughts, I scrambled over to the other side of the tree for a view of the small herd. Eight buffalo stood well within the bounds of the eagle closure. The calf was among the first newborns of the year, and I watched her intently, hoping that this small herd would remain in the closure for the rest of the day and somehow survive through spring. Shaky on her lanky legs, she stuck close to her mother, standing between the massive back legs and arching her neck to nurse. The wonder of this new life and the hope such a sight should engender were eclipsed by my sadness at the immediate situation. While this small herd would likely escape the day's capture, thanks to the delay caused by Charlie's lockdown, its future prospects weren't as hopeful.

The thought was punctuated by the whine of a distant snowmobile. I looked up just as a jumble of at least thirty buffalo burst from a line of trees a mile down the bluffs. Half a moment later, the agents appeared, revving their engines and shouting at the frightened animals. The horse-mounted agents came next, cantering along in the buffalo's tracks.

Without warning, like the top of a wave peeling away in a heavy offshore wind, a sliver of the herd broke off from the rest and circled back, eluding the agents and disappearing into a thick stand of trees. Sticking with the eighteen remaining animals, the pursuing agents were relentless. Anticipating the barbed-wire fence that runs perpendicular to the bluffs, the herd cut to the right toward a gap in the fence by the road. As the buffalo made for the opening in the fence, one of the Forest Service officials turned them around with a quick and piercing blast from an air horn.

Trapped between the sharp sound waves and the hounding agents, the buffalo bolted through the barbed wire, ripping whole sections of fence from the posts and tearing chunks of their flesh in the process. Once the buffalo were through the fence, the operation proceeded along the road toward the trap. The buffalo hung their tongues as they trudged past me, exhausted from the seven-mile run. They followed the road to its end in the capture facility's outer corral, and an agent swung the gate shut behind them.

The captive herd rushed through the trap's main corridor, trampling the ground where Charlie had been locked only an hour before. Buffalo rushed from one end of the trap to the other, back and forth, in a frantic search for daylight. They flowed in a single mass, like a sped-up tide, through the maze of pens. I cringed each time the walls bowed out, knowing that the animals were goring one another as they crammed their way around corners.

The captors weren't content with eighteen buffalo. As soon as the main gate was latched, the agents set out to recover the escapees, and I found myself alone with the security guard. The next twenty minutes were excruciating. I couldn't decide whether to hold my post in the tree or climb down and try to liberate the buffalo from the trap. I was fairly certain that the US Forest Service agents were watching me from the cattle guard, but I couldn't be sure. I looked from the trapped buffalo to the door that held them in, wondering if the agents had locked it. I knew I could get to the door before anyone could get to me, but if it was locked, my action would only accomplish a quick trip to jail. If it was open, I might be able to set them free. But with so many agents in the area, how long would their freedom last? Maybe they'd join the small herd in the eagle closure. Failing or succeeding, I'd end up in jail, and the police would confiscate the camera and all of the day's footage. I knew that most of the trapped buffalo would end up dead and that if they had any chance, it was with me. But it didn't feel right. I debated with myself until the agents reappeared, then admonished myself for missing the chance. When I saw the agents bound for the trap with seven more buffalo, I wanted to cry. "I'm sorry. I'm so sorry," I told the ones in the trap, as if I alone had engineered their present hell.

With twenty-five buffalo in the trap, the agents gathered to tell stories and share laughs over the day's adventures. While I couldn't make out their words, I could see their smiles and hear their laughter as they recounted events. One of the park rangers kept looking up at me, and I knew that my videotaping made him uneasy. He didn't want to be recorded in the company of the buffalo killers; perhaps I reminded him that he was helping to slaughter buffalo that he should be protecting. I stayed in the tree until the buffalo had been loaded onto trucks and shipped to the Duck Creek trap, where they would spend their last night on earth. I climbed down after the final trailer pulled away, and I walked toward the cattle guard.

I was surprised to see Charlie standing with the others, and as I walked toward him, I started to sob. It had been a long time since I'd cried for the buffalo; I had developed other ways of grieving. But the morning had been particularly difficult. Charlie had put his body on the line to save the buffalo. I wanted to tell him how much I admired his courage and that his action had been effective. The herd in the eagle closure could attest to that. With tears on my face and so many thoughts in my head, I hugged my brother. "Thank you, Charlie," I told him. "Thank you for doing that."

My friends filled me in on events I had missed from the tree. Charlie had been driven to town, cited for obstructing a government operation and trespassing, then released. Because he was a minor at the time (he would turn eighteen two weeks later), they couldn't hold him in jail. Another volunteer, Nick "Cookie" Cook, had been arrested by the US Forest Service officers at the cattle guard. After watching the buffalo tear themselves up in the fence, Cookie had turned to the officer who blew the air horn and shouted, "Why did you do that? Why did you push them through the fence?"

The officer, perhaps feeling a tinge of guilt for the buffalo injured in the fence, hadn't been open to critique. He had walked into the crowd of people gathered at the cattle guard, grabbed Cookie by the arm, and told him he was under arrest. When Cookie asked why, the officer said only "obstruction." Cookie had been standing with the other volunteers and, like them, had obeyed every order given by the law-enforcement officers. He hadn't attempted to disrupt the capture operation or interfere in any way. His only crime had been to question the actions of a public employee engaged in managing wildlife on public land. Cookie was transported 250 miles to the federal jail in Missoula, where he would be held until his arraignment the following day.

We sat on the sage flats talking about the things we'd just seen, shocked by the sudden peace and silence that seemed incongruous with the morning's events. The herd in the closure came down from the butte and stood in the road for awhile. I wondered if they could smell the fear of their brothers, sisters, and cousins who had just been captured.

I stood and walked over to the torn-up fence, finding tufts of hair and small, bloody chunks of hide tangled in the strands of barbed wire and lying on the ground nearby. I pictured the twenty-five buffalo in the livestock trailers being unloaded at Duck Creek. Given the winter's statistics (of the 119 bison captured, 53 had been released after testing negative for brucellosis antibodies), I was hopeful that at least some of the captive bison might be released.

My hope was unfounded, and the next two days were worse than I'd imagined possible. After transporting the buffalo to Duck Creek, the agents captured ten more buffalo there, bringing the day's total to thirty-five. At least one buffalo was shot after suffering a broken leg in confinement, and another gave birth in the Duck Creek trap. In their press release, DOL officials praised themselves for releasing the newborn calf and its mother. But somehow the DOL released the wrong cow and she quickly abandoned the small calf. Even after its mother had been shipped to slaughter with the rest of the herd, the small calf wouldn't leave the side of the trap. Each time a DOL agent carried it to the park, the calf just turned around and headed back in a desperate search for its mother. Orphaned on its first day of life, the tiny buffalo stood little chance of survival.

Of the thirty-five buffalo captured that day, the DOL killed thirty-four. Only the cow and new calf were spared. The day's operation marked a turning point in DOL policy. For the rest of the spring, all captured buffalo would be sent to slaughter without being tested for brucellosis. In the two weeks following the capture operation that Charlie had attempted to disrupt, 108 bison were captured. With the exception of seven that were captured, tested, tagged, and released earlier in the winter, all were sent to slaughter without testing. Neither the US Forest Service nor the National Park Service protested the DOL's decision to kill untested bison. The park's public-relations spokesperson, deflecting criticism of the park's involvement in the killing, said, "It's part of the plan that's been agreed to by all parties. That's just the way it is. It's an action that was consistent with the plan."

Since its signing in December 2000, the Interagency Bison Management Plan has been a favorite scapegoat of Yellowstone officials seeking to deflect blame for park involvement in the buffalo slaughter. When National Park Service personnel are criticized for participating in the slaughter, arresting protesters, or acquiescing to the DOL's decision to kill buffalo without testing them, their typical response is to blame the plan. This strategy belies the fact that the National Park Service was a lead agency in the plan's development and ultimately agreed to all of its management provisions.

The plan pays no respect to the Yellowstone buffalo's significance as a singularly wild, genetically distinct population. While most of the 500,000 living bison possess cattle genes, the Yellowstone herd does not. Scientists believe that less than 5,000 genetically pure bison remain in the world. According to recent genetic studies of hundreds of private herds and virtually every public herd, the Yellowstone population is the largest, and likely the only, population of genetically pure bison remaining. "The random shooting at the Montana border," another scientist warned, is causing "an irreversible crippling of the gene pool." The plan gives lip service to the importance of the herd but does nothing to protect its cultural, historical, or genetic importance.

The result of ten years of legal wrangling between the federal government and the state of Montana, the bison-management plan is more the result of politics than science. Work on the plan began in 1990 and lurched along slowly as the so-called "cooperating" agencies squabbled at every turn.

The Park Service and the DOL—agencies with radically different mandates—had trouble agreeing on anything. It took more than seven years just to draft the plan's stated objectives, a vaguely worded marriage of principles that reflect the agencies' differing viewpoints:

> *The purpose of the proposed interagency action is to maintain a wild, free-ranging population of bison and address the risk of brucellosis transmission to protect the economic interest and viability of the livestock industry in the state of Montana.*

The agencies continued to work out the details of the final plan until 1999, when federal officials, concerned that the state was unnecessarily committed to slaughtering bison, pulled out of the negotiations. A spokesman for APHIS said at the time, "We don't feel there's a need to kill every bison that comes out of the park." A judge overseeing the process ordered the state and federal governments to keep working, and eventually an agreement was reached; the plan was signed in December 2000.

Implementation of the plan, set to be in effect until 2015, is costing taxpayers more than three million dollars a year. One example of the plan's disrespect for the wild qualities that make the Yellowstone herd unique is the provision for the insertion of vaginal telemetry devices and radio collars in all captured, pregnant bison. The transmitters are designed to be expelled when the buffalo give birth, allowing management agencies to test the birth sites for *Brucella*, the bacterium that causes brucellosis. If the bacteria are present, the buffalo cow and its newborn calf are tracked down and shot.

The plan mandates that captured buffalo be blood tested for brucellosis antibodies. Those possessing antibodies are slaughtered. Because the test determines only the presence of antibodies and not the disease itself, perfectly healthy bison with no chance of transmitting brucellosis will continue to be slaughtered. This is like killing everyone who has been immunized to polio in an attempt to eradicate the disease.

A tissue-culture test, performed after slaughter, determines actual infection. National Park Service biologist Mary Meagher and Professor

Mary Meyer, two of the world's leading experts on bison and brucellosis, wrote:

> *Although more than 50% of Yellowstone's bison test positive for Brucella antibodies through blood tests, tissue culture tests—ordinarily viewed as a more reliable testing protocol for identifying active infection—indicate a much lower infection rate.*

Tests conducted by APHIS confirm the shortcomings of the blood test. Of 144 bison that were shot or sent to slaughter between January 1997 and April 1999 based on blood-test results, only twenty-six cultures tested positive. Eighty-two percent of the slaughtered bison (118 individuals) showed no trace of brucellosis. Management agencies abandoned culture tests during the winter of 2001–2, making it impossible for critics to ascertain the number of brucellosis-negative bison being slaughtered.

In addition to the existing traps at Horse Butte, Duck Creek, and one inside the park at Stephens Creek, the plan has resulted in the construction of new traps and quarantine facilities—large holding pens where bison testing negative are confined for ten years or longer.

The plan places an arbitrary population cap of 3,000 animals on the herd. This provision was cited by the DOL during the spring of 2002 when the agency slaughtered 135 bison without testing. While National Park Service officials acknowledge that the cap was politically rather than ecologically derived, they nonetheless agreed to it. The park hasn't always acquiesced so readily to the whims of the livestock industry. In the year of negotiations leading up to the signing of the plan, park officials were openly critical of DOL actions. Mike Finley, Yellowstone superintendent from 1994 to 2001, had strong words for the DOL during an interview with ABC's *Nightline* ("Buffalo Wars," conducted by Chris Bury) that aired on February 9, 2000:

> *Some poor bull bison stepped outside and crossed this imaginary line looking for a blade of grass, and then someone either shoots him or*

drives around on a snowmobile and says, "We're just protecting the
cattle industry." That doesn't sell. That doesn't sell anywhere.

During the winter of 1996–97, park rangers showed their disdain for
Park Service participation in the slaughter by wearing black armbands.
Ranger Tom Mazzarisi condemned the livestock industry and complacent
Park Service personnel in the August 21, 1998, issue of the *Yellowstone
Net Newsletter*:

> *Do not allow the livestock industry to have control of our nation's
> wildlife, because our wildlife will be treated like cattle, as is the case
> with buffalo right now. It is our duty as American citizens and those
> who earn their livings providing visitors with Yellowstone memories to
> support the buffalo. It is unconscionable and hypocritical to hear of
> those who favor and participate in the slaughter of buffalo and at the
> same time take millions of dollars from visitors.*

Mazzarisi's views are more in keeping with the park's original
mandate than with the views of the current managers. Whereas the park
rangers who assist the DOL are being paid to support the politically
motivated decisions of their superiors and defend the livestock-industry-
induced slaughter, early park managers acted out of a sense of what was
right for the park and its geological and biological features. The present
bison-management plan contrasts with the original legislation creating
Yellowstone National Park, which provides that wildlife should not be
"wantonly destroyed" nor subject to "capture and destruction for the pur-
poses of merchandise or profit."

Early park rangers and administrators, recognizing Yellowstone's
unique role as the last harbor of wild bison in the country, went to great
lengths to protect bison from the poachers who killed them. The selfless dili-
gence of Acting Superintendent George Anderson and backcountry scout
Felix Burgess in February 1894 led to the capture of a notorious poacher and
spurred one of the most significant pieces of legislation in park history.

Without these early advocates, wild American buffalo would likely have died with the nineteenth century.

Poacher Edgar Howell had set up camp in Yellowstone's remote Pelican Valley during the fall and winter of 1893–94 and was engaged in killing some of the park's last remaining buffalo. Howell had snowshoed into the park's interior from Cooke City in September, hauling a 180-pound supply sled, and had made his home in the park for the winter. Planning on selling the increasingly rare heads to collectors, his enterprise was foiled when Burgess, on a winter ski patrol funded by Anderson's personal savings, captured him in the act of slaughtering five buffalo.

Burgess, suffering frostbite that would result in the amputation of his big toe, made a stealthy and daring approach across an open snowfield to get within pistol range of Howell and his dog, neither of whom detected him. The poacher surrendered and was escorted to the town of Mammoth on an excruciatingly long and bitter February ski across some of the coldest and least hospitable terrain in the country. At the time, there was no enforceable law against poaching in Yellowstone; all the scouts could do was escort Howell to the park boundary.

Fortuitously, a reporter from *Field and Stream* happened to be visiting the park at the time of Howell's apprehension. Emerson Hough met Howell and his captors as they made their way through the park, interviewed the involved parties, and wrote a story that he rushed to his publisher, George Bird Grinnell, in New York. The story generated such public outcry against poaching that legislation "to protect the birds and animals in Yellowstone National Park" was soon enacted. The Lacey Act of May 1894 finally gave park managers the legal and jurisdictional authority to prosecute poachers, allowing the bison to survive into the twentieth century.

The National Park Service's present-day involvement in the capture and slaughter of buffalo is inconsistent with Yellowstone's enacting legislation and jeopardizes the achievements of the park's nineteenth-century defenders. Where park personnel once were charged with apprehending bison killers, today they are more likely to be found arresting citizens for performing acts of civil disobedience aimed at protecting the buffalo.

This new role, in which rangers who joined the Park Service to protect wildlife find themselves helping to kill bison, makes many of them uneasy. One ranger volunteers with Buffalo Field Campaign—risking his job in the process—whenever he has a few days off. Other rangers say that they are thankful for our work and are uncomfortable with the buffalo-related aspects of their own. Before the plan was signed, some of these rangers would help us walk buffalo to safe areas to prevent their capture at the hands of the DOL.

But with the new plan in place, National Park Service personnel are required to assist the DOL with operations on both sides of the park boundary. For many rangers, this means engaging in activities to which they have strong moral objections. These people know that the buffalo slaughter is wrong, yet they must continue to follow orders from their superiors and help haze, capture, test, and ship buffalo to slaughter.

In his essay "Civil Disobedience," Henry David Thoreau called such people "wooden men" and "machines," noting that, in their actions, "there is no free exercise whatever of the judgement or of the moral sense." He also noted that they are often touted as being good citizens for their obedience to rules and laws that they find unconscionable. Wildlife-loving park rangers engaged in buffalo slaughter justify their actions primarily on the basis of job security, convincing themselves that they need the money. Or they justify their actions against beneficial work in other aspects of park management, calling the buffalo slaughter a necessary evil.

"Get a job!" is a refrain to which we are accustomed, as everyone from park rangers to DOL agents harangue us for our efforts to protect the buffalo. No matter how many times I try to explain myself to them, these men don't understand it when I tell them that I have a job, even though its wages do not come in the form of a paycheck. Right livelihood, it seems, is an unfamiliar concept to these men. They don't understand how the work can be its own reward. Like the early park scouts and administrators—underfunded and overworked—those of us working to protect the buffalo are driven by our love of the wild land and what we know to be right.

"Unjust laws exist," Thoreau wrote. "Shall we be content to obey them,

or shall we endeavor to amend them, and obey them until we have suc-
ceeded, or shall we transgress them at once?"

Kneeling in the grass and sage, plucking tufts of buffalo hair from the
base of a barbed-wire fence, I considered Thoreau's question on the afternoon of Charlie's arrest. The DOL, Park Service, and Forest Service agents
haven't left us a choice. Their intentions were laid bare in 1997 with the
slaughter of nearly 1,100 buffalo. Working through the system has its place.
Submitting public comments, signing petitions, filing lawsuits, organizing
rallies, and meeting with public officials are all ways of effecting change.
Constructing blockades, placing one's body between the buffalo and the
rifles, locking to the capture facility, and documenting the slaughter are
other ways. Each is useful and effective under the right circumstances at the
right time.

The buffalo slaughter of 2002 received almost no media attention until
a volunteer blockaded the road accessing the Horse Butte trap. His arrest
generated a national Associated Press story and an article in the *New York
Times*. Readers contacted Buffalo Field Campaign, wrote letters to elected
officials, and began learning about the buffalo. The slaughter will only abate
when enough people know the truth and demand that the government
respect the right of the last wild buffalo to utilize the lands, inside and outside the park, that they need for survival.

I combed a tuft of buffalo hair from the grass at the base of the fence
and raised it to my face. Pressing my nose into the downy fur, I closed my
eyes and inhaled its musky scent. The black and curly hair made me think of
my mother. Ten years had passed since she visited me in the dream, giving
me the confidence to continue on my difficult course. "The path you are on
is right," she had said. When I began working with the campaign, I was
naïve. I thought it would take a year, maybe two, to raise enough public pressure to stop the slaughter. More than fifteen years have passed, and, with the
park's increasing complicity in the kill, the end seems farther away than it
was when I started. "Discouraged" is a far too gentle word for the way I feel
after watching yet another slaughter. Friends spend months in jail for their
brave and noble actions, and it sometimes seems that we are wasting our

time. But if we weren't out here, who would monitor the actions of the DOL? Who would share with the world the buffalo's story? I get discouraged sometimes and feel like giving up, but the buffalo have a way of bringing me back to my senses.

———

One spring day when no buffalo were killed, I hiked out to Horse Butte by myself with a bundle of sage. It was the anniversary of a particularly bad killing, and I wanted to pray for the buffalo that had been sent to slaughter. Sitting on the bluffs near the trap, I remembered beautiful days with the buffalo, and days of capture. I fished a lighter from my pocket and lit the sage. All of the memories melded together.

A breeze blew up from the river and carried a thread of smoke from the sage bundle out across the flats toward the trap. I visualized mass upon brown mass of buffalo flowing toward the trap and felt the deep bass rumble of their hooves in the earth. Closing my eyes, I pictured the smirking DOL agents riding horses, snowmobiles, and four-wheelers, hounding the animals with cracker rounds and shouting "Haauw!" as they stuffed the buffalo into the steel trap. I pictured, one by one, the faces of various friends who were hauled off to jail by the livestock agents over the years.

Many winters with the buffalo flashed before my eyes, winters of skiing out in the subfreezing dawn, winters of watching some of the same buffalo graze in the same meadows, winters of watching them die. I felt fresh the claustrophobia of being hemmed in beside the barbed-wire fence and the cattle guard by agents threatening arrest. I heard the echoes of my friends shouting, "Run! Run! Run!" when it looked like buffalo would bypass the trap and drop down the bluffs to the safety of the Madison River. I thought back to that spring day in 1999 when I watched a herd of buffalo, on their way to capture, hesitate on the brink of the bluff, allowing the agents to circle around them and chase them back into the open mouth of the trap. I imagined the rattling of the trap's panels in its hinges as seventy buffalo spent their last days and nights in terrified confinement. I saw trailer after trailer, heavy with their cargoes of doomed buffalo, disappear down the road on the way to the slaughterhouse.

Kneeling in the meadow, burning sage for all of the buffalo I'd seen killed over the years, I wondered when the killing would end for good and how I could hasten the day. I heard a rustling of grass from the bluffs and looked up just as a herd of thirty buffalo crested the rim. I knew I was in the right place as the slow-moving, grass-munching cows and calves approached. I wasn't scared and I held still.

Ten feet from me, the herd parted, half passing to my east and half to my west. I stayed where I was, burning the sage. Soon I was surrounded, sitting in the center of the small herd. Never had I been so close to so many buffalo. In that moment, I was certain that they knew who I was and why I was there. Sitting in the center of the circle, I listened to the sharp snap and crunch of hundreds of blades of grass. Sage smoke drifted from my hand to the nose of a pregnant cow, who lifted her head and stared straight into my eyes. I sat in amazement, surrounded, drawing strength for the work that lay ahead.

Notes and Sources

Chapter One ∞ Breaking Trail

Information on the cultural history of the Head Smashed In Buffalo Jump is from Barney Reeves, "Six Millenniums of Buffalo Kills," *Scientific American*, October 1983, vol. 249 (4), p. 122.

Much of my knowledge on the distribution of buffalo jumps and their impracticality in the warmer climates of the Southern Plains is from Dan Flores's excellent graduate history course, "Indian, Bison, and Horse," taught at the University of Montana, and particularly his "Ancient Hunters" lecture on February 20, 2001.

General information on Head Smashed In and the meaning of the Blackfeet word *Piskun* as "deep blood kettle" is from: George Arthur, *An Introduction to the Ecology of Early Historic Communal Bison Hunting on the Northern Plains*, Archaeological Survey of Canada, Paper #37, pp. 74–75.

In addition to Arthur (*Ecology of Early Historic Communal Bison Hunting*) and Reeves ("Six Millenniums of Buffalo Kills"), I learned a great deal about the Head Smashed In site from Liz Bryan's well-written and informative *The Buffalo People*, University of Alberta Press, Edmonton, 1991, pp. 49–52.

There is much debate on the number of bison inhabiting the plains at the time of European contact. Many of the twentieth-century estimates were as high as 75 million. See, for example, Ernest Thompson Seton, *Life Histories of Northern Animals*, vol. 1, New York, 1910, p. 292.

More recent studies based on a combination of historical accounts and ecological studies of the carrying capacity of the Great Plains place the number closer to 25 million. See Dan Flores, "Bison Ecology and Bison Diplomacy," *The Journal of American History*, September 1991, p. 471.

The source for my information on the last use of the buffalo jump occurring around 1850 is from Arthur, *Ecology of Early Historic Communal Bison Hunting*, p. 72.

Information on the importance of Pelican Valley to the history of Yellowstone bison is from Mary Meagher, *The Bison of Yellowstone National Park*, National Park Service, 1973, p. 17.

Information on the origins of the bison imported into Yellowstone National Park can be found in *Superintendent of the Yellowstone National Park*, "Annual Report," Yellowstone National Park Library, 1902.

Paul Schullery's *Yellowstone's Ski Pioneers* (High Plains Publishing, Worland, Wyo., 1995, p. 116) also has good information on the early history of Yellowstone buffalo.

I first learned about the roles of Samuel Walking Coyote and Charles and Mary Goodnight in preserving the species in David Dary's encyclopedic *The Buffalo Book* (Avon Books, New York, 1974, p. 222). Kenneth Zontec's "Saving the Bison: The Story of Samuel Walking Coyote" (unpublished master's thesis, New Mexico State University, 1993, Chapter 3) provided a deeper understanding.

Information on the Goodnights' role in preserving the bison is from Evetts Haley, *Charles Goodnight: Cowman and Plainsman*, University of Oklahoma Press, Norman, 1949, p. 439.

My discussion of the singularity of the Yellowstone bison and the origins of the present herd, including the differences between plains and mountain bison, is informed by Meagher, *The Bison of Yellowstone National Park*, p. 26.

Numbers of bison killed during the winter of 1996–97 are from: United States Department of the Interior, National Park Service, *Bison Management Plan for the State of Montana and Yellowstone National Park*, Final Environmental Impact Statement, August 8, 2000, vol. I, p. 379.

Information on the New England cod fishery is from Farley Mowat, *Sea of Slaughter*, Bantam Books, New York, 1986, p. 166.

Documentation of the lack of brucellosis transmission from bison to livestock is from the National Research Council, *Brucellosis in the Greater Yellowstone Area*, National Academy of Sciences Press, Washington, D.C., 1998, p. 45.

Mary Meagher's description of the Yellowstone bison as "wild and unfettered" is from Meagher, *The Bison of Yellowstone National Park*, p. 12.

Chapter Two ∾ Negligent Endangerment

Photos of the skull and bone "mountains" can be found in Dary, *The Buffalo Book*, pp. 138–139.

Theodore Davis's description of shooting buffalo from trains is from "The Buffalo Range," *Harper's Monthly*, January 1869, vol. 38, p. 149.

"Buffalo" Bill Cody's exploits are recounted in William Hornaday, *The Extermination of the American Bison*, Smithsonian Institution, Washington, D.C., 1889, p. 478.

Claims that brucellosis threatens Montana's economy can be found in Montana Department of Livestock and Montana Department of Fish, Wildlife, and Parks, "Interagency Bison Management Plan for the State of Montana and Yellowstone National Park: Record of Decision," State of Montana, Helena, December 20, 2000, p. 1.

For an example of Montana's claims that bison threaten the state's economy, see Karen Cooper, "Third Season of Interagency Bison Management Plan Underway," press release, Montana Department of Livestock, November 21, 2002.

Information on Grand Teton National Park, where bison and cattle have coexisted since 1950, is drawn from the following sources: Virginia Ravndal, personal interview, October 1999; Todd Wilkenson, "To the South, Bison and Cattle Coexist," *High Country News*, February 17, 1997 (http://www.hcn.org/issues/99/3061); and Whitney Royster, "Grand Teton Chief: Grazing Might Continue," *Casper Star Tribune*, September 16, 2004 (http://trib.com/news/state-and-regional/article_393884f9-feb3-5b5b-a22b-0c15cd0f3d54.html).

The details of cattle and bison intermingling near Gardiner in 1989 are from Robert Keiter, "Greater Yellowstone's Bison: Unraveling of an Early American Wildlife Conservation Achievement," *Journal of Wildlife Management*, January 1997, vol. 61, p. 4.

The scientific conclusion that bison pose no threat of transmitting brucellosis to cattle is from the United States Congress's General Accounting Office, "Wildlife Management: Many Issues Unresolved in Yellowstone Bison-Cattle Conflict," GAO Report RCED-93-2, US Government Printing Office, Washington, D.C., 1992.

The National Research Council reached a similar conclusion in *Brucellosis in the Greater Yellowstone Area*, National Academy of Sciences Press, Washington, D.C., 1998, p. 80.

NPS biologist John Mack is quoted in George Wuerthner, "The Battle Over Bison," *National Parks*, November–December 1995, p. 39.

Dr. Paul Nicolletti is quoted in Dan Brister and Mike Mease, *Buffalo Bull* (video documentary), Cold Mountain, Cold Rivers, Missoula, Mont., 1998.

A list of species in the Yellowstone area carrying brucellosis can be found in National Research Council, *Brucellosis in the Greater Yellowstone Area*, pp. 37–41.

Jay Kirkpatrick's quote about the double standard for elk versus bison is from his "Trouble Where the Bison Roam," *The Quarterly Journal of In Defense of Endangered Species*, Winter 1992, pp. 4–10.

Patrick Collins, from USDA APHIS, is quoted in Joe Kolman, "Feds Pull Out of Bison Talks with Montana," *Billings Gazette*, December 16, 1999, p. 1.

Figures on the number of cattle that use lands that are seasonally grazed by bison can be found in the United States Congress's General Accounting Office, *Wildlife Management: Negotiations on a Long-Term Plan for Managing Yellowstone Bison Still Ongoing*, GAO/RCED-00-7, p. 4.

A more recent examination of the number of cattle in the area can be found in A. Marm Kilpatrick, Colin Gillin, and Peter Daszak, "Wildlife–Livestock Conflict: The Risk of Pathogen Transmission from Bison to Cattle Outside Yellowstone National Park," *Journal of Applied Ecology*, British Ecological Society, 2009, p. 3.

The quote from the Wyoming Game and Fish employee on the livestock industry's true motivation for slaughtering bison is from Wuerthner, "The Battle Over Bison," p. 39.

John Varley's characterization of the bison slaughter as a struggle between

Yellowstone National Park and agribusiness is from Doug Peacock, "The Yellowstone Massacre," *Audubon*, May–June 1997, p. 43.

The Idaho rancher who believes bison should be kept inside Yellowstone was quoted in Scott McMillion, "Suit Aimed at Grazing Lease in Bison Country," *Bozeman Daily Chronicle*, July 11, 2001.

Montana Code 81-2-120 permits the Department of Livestock to auction the remains of bison and keep the proceeds.

Figures on the amount of money raised by the Department of Livestock through the sale of slaughtered bison are from Mac Corelli, Department of Livestock subcontractor, interviewed in Dan Brister and Mike Mease, *Buffalo Bull* (video documentary), Cold Mountain, Cold Rivers, Missoula, Mont., 1998.

Facts on the buffalo illegally killed by Dale Koelzer are from Scott McMillion, "No Open Season on Bison, Judge Rules," *Bozeman Daily Chronicle*, January 29, 2000, and Joan Haines, "Koelzer Found Guilty Only of Wasting Game Meat," *Bozeman Daily Chronicle*, July 6, 2000.

Chapter Three ∾ Inseparable Destiny

"In life and death we and the buffalo have always shared the same fate." This quote is from John Fire Lame Deer and Richard Erdoes, *Lame Deer: Seeker of Visions,* Simon and Schuster, New York, 1972, p. 244.

Linda Hogan's quotation is from an interview with Derrick Jensen in *Listening to the Land: Conversations About Nature, Culture, and Eros*, Sierra Club Books, San Francisco, 1995, p. 123.

Rosalie Little Thunder recounted the story of her arrest and her family's connection to the Sand Creek Massacre in her "Letter to Chris Kelley of the Church Universal and Triumphant," May 1997.

The horrors of the Sand Creek Massacre and its aftermath are recounted in: United States Congress, "Joint Committee on the Conduct of the War Massacre of Cheyenne Indians," Thirty-Eighth Congress, Second Session, 1865, p. 6; George Bird Grinnell, *The Fighting Cheyennes*, University of Oklahoma Press, Norman, 1956, pp. 170–174; Duane Schultz, *Month of the Freezing Moon: The Sand Creek Massacre*, St. Martin's Press, New York, 1990, pp. 134–146; and John Stands in Timber and Margaret Liberty, *Cheyenne Memories*, University of Nebraska Press, Lincoln, 1967, p. 169.

The quotes from Rosalie Little Thunder on her arrest and her family's connection to the Sand Creek Massacre and the attack on Chief Little Thunder's band are from: Winona LaDuke, *All Our Relations: Native Struggles for Land and Life*, South End Press, Cambridge, 1999, pp. 154–155; Patricia Walsh, "Slaughter of Bison Reopens Old Wounds," *High Country News* 29(11), June 9, 1997; Rosalie Little Thunder, personal interview, November 2, 1999; and Dan Brister and Mike Mease, *Buffalo Bull* (video documentary), Cold Mountain, Cold Rivers, Missoula, Mont., 1998.

Fred Dubray's quotation on the tendency to destroy that which we fear is from United States Department of the Interior, National Park Service, *Bison Management Plan for the State of Montana and Yellowstone National Park, Volume Three: Responses to Comments on the Draft Environmental Impact Statement*, December 2000, p. 810.

Scott Frazier recounted the Crow creation story at Buffalo Field Campaign's nightly meeting on November 11, 1999.

Mari Sandoz wrote about the Pawnee creation story in *The Buffalo Hunters*, University of Nebraska Press, Lincoln, 1954, p. ix.

The Crow creation account is from Plenty Coups and Frank Linderman, editor, *The Life Story of a Great Indian, Plenty Coups, Chief of the Crows,* University of Nebraska Press, Lincoln, 1930, p. 63.

Greg Bourland's telling of the Lakota creation story is recounted in *Bison Management Plan for the State of Montana and Yellowstone National Park, Volume Three: Responses to Comments on the Draft Environmental Impact Statement,* p. 762.

John Fire Lame Deer's quotation that begins "The buffalo was part of us . . ." is from Lame Deer and Richard Erdoes, *Lame Deer,* p. 244; his telling of the many uses of buffalo in virtually every aspect of Lakota life can be found on p. 119.

General Sheridan's "If I could learn that every buffalo in the northern herd were killed I would be glad . . ." quotation is from General Phil Sheridan, "Letter to Adjutant General," October 13, 1881, Box 29, Sheridan Papers, cited in Paul Hutton, *Phil Sheridan and His Army,* University of Nebraska Press, Lincoln, 1985, p. 246.

Columbus Delano's pronouncement that "The civilization of the Indian is impossible while the buffalo remains upon the plains..." is from the "Annual Report of the Secretary of Interior," 1873. My source for this quote is Dary, *The Buffalo Book,* p. 127.

James Throckmorton's argument that "so long as there are millions of buffaloes in the West, the Indians cannot be controlled" is found in the Congressional Record, 1876. It is cited in Valerius Geist, *Buffalo Nation: History and Legend of the North American Bison,* Voyageur Press, Stillwater, Minn., 1996, p. 84.

James Mooar tells the story of Colonel Richard Dodge telling him " . . . hunt where the buffalo are..." in his essay, "The First Buffalo Hunting in the

Panhandle," *West Texas Historical Association Yearbook*, vol. 6, 1930, pp. 109–110. It is also cited in Dary, *The Buffalo Book*, p. 108.

Chasing Hawk's quotation on the killing of Yellowstone buffalo being akin to the killing of his people's brothers and sisters is from *Bison Management Plan for the State of Montana and Yellowstone National Park, Volume Three: Responses to Comments on the Draft Environmental Impact Statement*, p. 759.

Rosalie Little Thunder's comparison of the killing of buffalo during the Gardiner prayer ceremony to "a murder in the church parking lot during the service" is quoted by Walsh, "Slaughter of Bison Reopens New Wounds," p. 1.

Information on White Buffalo Calf Woman and the origins of the sacred Lakota pipe bundle are from Lame Deer and Richard Erdoes, *Lame Deer*, p. 243.

Corey Mascio described his arrest to me in a personal interview conducted on February 23, 1998.

President Clinton's executive order on tribal representation in matters affecting tribal cultures can be found in the *Federal Register*, Executive Order of May 1998, Section 3, "Consultation."

James Garrett's statement on "mixing consultation with insultation" is from Winona LaDuke, "Buffalo: Winter Comes to Yellowstone," *News from Indian Country: The Independent Native Journal*, Special Edition: Millennium 2000, pp. B1–B8.

Fred Dubray's thoughts on his people being excluded from management decisions can be found in *Bison Management Plan for the State of Montana and Yellowstone National Park, Volume Three: Responses to Comments on the Draft Environmental Impact Statement*, p. 757.

Chapter Four ∽ Cattle and Control: A History of Western Violence

Faulkner's famous "The past is never dead . . . " quote is from William Faulkner, "Requiem for a Nun," Random House, New York, 1951.

For a recent estimate on the number of bison that once inhabited North America, see Dan Flores, "Bison Ecology and Bison Diplomacy," *The Journal of American History*, September 1991, p. 471.

North America's historical buffalo population comprised the largest concentration of animals known to exist, according to Lynn Jacobs, *Waste of the West: Public Lands Ranching*, Lynn Jacobs Press, Tucson, 1991, p. 114.

The quotation comparing the number of bison to the number of leaves in a forest is from William Hornaday, *The Extermination of the American Bison*, US Government Printing Office, 1889, p. 387.

Information on F. F. Gerard's estimate that a million and a half buffalo were killed in the upper Missouri region in 1857 is from David Dary, *The Buffalo Book*, p, 78.

The many uses of buffalo robes are cataloged in David Dary, *The Buffalo Book*, p. 88.

Information on William "Buffalo Bill" Cody and the role of the railroads in decimating the great herds is also from David Dary, *The Buffalo Book*, pp. 83–85.

Charles Wilkinson discusses the rapid rise of cattle on the plains in the wake of the buffalos' disappearance in *Crossing the Next Meridian*, Island Press, Washington, D.C., 1992, p. 82.

The number of cattle driven north from Texas to the railroad depots between 1866 and 1884 can be found in Rodman Paul, *The Far West and the Great Plains in Transition 1859–1900*, Harper & Row, New York, 1988, p. 195.

For a firsthand account detailing the extensive number of Texas cattle in Kansas in 1867, see Francis Haines, *The Buffalo*, Apollo Editions, New York, 1975, p. 173.

William Cronon documents the replacement of bison with cattle as the dominant grazer on the Great Plains in *Nature's Metropolis: Chicago and the Great West*, Norton, New York, 1991, p. 220.

Richard Dodge writes about cattle replacing buffalo in *Our Wild Indians: Thirty-Three Years' Personal Experience Among the Red Men of the Great West*, A.D. Worthington and Company, 1886, pp. 608–609.

My source for four and a half million buffalo being slaughtered between 1882 and 1884 is Frank Mayer and Charles Roth, *The Buffalo Harvest*, Sage Books, Denver, 1958, p. 87.

The quotation on the delivery of nearly 40 million pounds of beef to thirty-four Indian reservations is from Maurice Frink, *When Grass Was King*, University of Colorado Press, Boulder, 1956, p. 13.

Granville Stuart's firsthand account of the valleys being "sprinkled with the carcasses of dead buffalo" is from Granville Stuart, *Forty Years on the Frontier*, vol. II, Arthur H. Clark Company, Cleveland, 1925, p. 104.

General Nelson Miles's prescient observation that cattle would take the place of buffalo and Indians was recorded in Mark Brown and W. Felton, *Before Barbed Wire*, Henry Holt, New York, 1956, p. 98.

Parkman predicted that the "buffalo [would] give place to tame cattle" in Francis Parkman, *The Oregon Trail*, 8th ed., Little, Brown, Boston, 1872.

I originally learned of the vigilante roots behind Montana's cryptic 3-7-77 from Don Spritzer, *A Roadside History of Montana*, Mountain Press Publishing Company, Missoula, Mont., 1999, p. 237.

For a more detailed examination of this symbology, see Frederick Allen, "Montana Vigilantes and the Origins of 3-7-77," *Montana: The Magazine of Western History*, Spring 2001, pp. 1–19.

Granville Stuart argued that livestock inspectors should be granted the power to arrest citizens in his "Letter to Preston Leslie, Governor of the Territory of Montana," Office of the Territorial Board of Stock Commissioners, February 10, 1887.

For background on the roots of the conflict between stockmen and homesteaders, see Mari Sandoz, *The Cattlemen*, University of Nebraska Press, Lincoln, 1958, p. 337.

Mari Sandoz discusses the "Big Die Up" in *The Cattlemen*, pp. 259–271. She writes about the cattle barons and livestock associations targeting settlers on p. 332.

For specific details on the cattle wars, see Wilkinson, *Crossing the Next Meridian*, p. 86, and Helena Smith, *The War on Powder River: The History of an Insurrection*, University of Nebraska Press, Lincoln, 1966, p. 164.

The power of the Wyoming Stockgrowers Association and its role as organizer of the Johnson County invasion is chronicled in Helena Smith, *The War on Powder River*, p. 275.

Mari Sandoz writes about the recruiting of the invading army, their pay, and how they were armed with guns from the state arsenal in *The Cattlemen*, pp. 357–359.

My source for the fifty-dollar bounty the invaders were promised for each confirmed kill and the $100,000 price tag of the invasion is Helena Smith, *The War on Powder River*, pp. 191–192.

Composition of the Stockgrowers' hit list is discussed by Mari Sandoz, *The Cattlemen*, p. 359, and Helena Smith, *The War on Powder River*, p. 194.

Members of the invading army, their weaponry, and supplies are documented by Helena Smith, *The War on Powder River*, p. 196, and Bill O'Neil, *Cattlemen vs. Sheepherders: Five Decades of Violence in the West*, Eakin Press, Austin, Texas, 1989, p. 91.

Nate Champion's journal entry was quoted by A. S. Mercer, *The Banditti of the Plains*, University of Oklahoma Press, Norman, 1954, p. 60.

The invaders' plan to blow up the Buffalo courthouse and shoot those who fled, as well as the role of Buffalo's citizens in suppressing the invasion, the invaders' surrender, and the lack of legal recourse, is detailed in Mari Sandoz, *The Cattlemen*, p. 361.

The exploits of "Stuart's Stranglers" are explored in Mari Sandoz, *The Cattlemen*, p. 500; Harry Drago, *The Great Range Wars: Violence on the Grasslands*, Dodd, Mead & Company, New York, 1970, pp. 226–231; and Montana Stockgrowers Association, "Early Days of the MSGA," p. 10.

The Cattle/Sheep Wars are discussed in detail by Bill O'Neil, *Cattlemen vs. Sheepherders*, p. 2, and Ogden Tanner, The Ranchers, Time-Life Books, Alexandria, Virginia, 1977, p. 120.

Information on the Bear Creak Raid is from Bill O'Neil, *Cattlemen vs. Sheepherders*, p. 71, and Lyman Brewster, "December, 1900: The Quiet Slaughter," *Montana: The Magazine of Western History*, Winter 1974, pp. 82–85.

The subsequent political careers of John Kendrick and George Brewster are discussed by Bill O'Neil, *Cattlemen vs. Sheepherders*, pp. 71–72.

The bounties paid by Montana on 81,000 wolves between 1883 and 1918 are discussed by Lynn Jacobs, *Waste of the West*, p. 270.

Information on the killing of wolves, coyotes, and mountain lions by the USDA's Biological Survey is from Denzel Ferguson and Nancy Ferguson, *Sacred Cows at the Public Trough*, Maverick Publications, Bend, Ore., 1983, p. 132, and Sharman Russell, *Kill the Cowboy: A Battle of Mythology in the New West*, Addison-Wesley Publishing Company, 1993, p. 75.

The quotation on "using public funds to kill publicly owned animals on public lands for the economic gain of private stockmen" is from Denzel Ferguson and Nancy Ferguson, *Sacred Cows at the Public Trough*, p. 133.

Background on the USDA's division of Animal Damage Control (ADC) and the livestock industry's lobbying to kill not just predators but perceived competitors is from Sharman Russell, *Kill the Cowboy*, p. 75.

Information on the "coyote getter," Compound 1080, and the dropping of millions of pieces of poisoned meat is from Denzel Ferguson and Nancy Ferguson, *Sacred Cows at the Public Trough*, p. 136.

The ADC figures of having killed at least 809,000 animals are cited in Denzel Ferguson and Nancy Ferguson, *Sacred Cows at the Public Trough*, p. 79.

The ADC agent who speaks of killing "so many coyotes I got ashamed of myself . . ." is quoted in Lynn Jacobs, *Waste of the West*, p. 263.

The idea of ranchers being in a state of perpetual warfare with the land was articulated by George Wuerthner in "Livestock: Myth & Reality," http://www.westernwatersheds.org/facts_photos/livestck_myths/livestck_myths.html (retrieved 4 October, 2011).

Bob Peebles expressed gratitude at being a "product of the raping era" during a presentation he made to the University of Montana Transboundary Environmental Issues Course, August 2000.

The "Rustling is still a capital offense" placard was noted by Sam Verhovek, "Band of Nevada Ranchers Clash with Government on Cattle Grazing Fees," *New York Times*, August 2, 2001.

Information on the death threats that Don Oman received is from Timothy Egan, "Ranchers vs. Rangers Over Land Use," *New York Times*, August 19 1990, Section 1, p. 20, and Sharman Russell, *Kill the Cowboy*, pp. 46, 50.

The ecological effects of overgrazing are documented by Thomas Fleischner, "Ecological Costs of Livestock Grazing in Western North America," *Conservation Biology*, September 1994, 8(3): pp. 629–644.

The comparisons showing Montana's relative lack of importance as a cattle grazing area are from Matthew Dietz, "Managing Public Lands to Support Viable Wildlife Populations in Montana's High Plains: The Montana High Plains Ecosystem Recovery Plan," master's thesis, University of Montana, 1995, p. 20.

The more general comparisons showing that the West is not the ideal place to raise domestic livestock are from Paul Rogers and Jennifer LaFleur,

"The Giveaway of the West: A Mercury News Special Report," *San Jose Mercury News*, November 7, 1999.

The findings of the US Congress's 1991 GAO Report are summarized in Matthew Dietz, "Managing Public Lands," p. 21.

Paul Rogers and Jennifer LaFleur detail the extent of grazing subsidies enjoyed by public-lands ranchers.

Figures on the percentages and total acreages of public lands that are grazed by cattle are from Sharman Russell, *Kill the Cowboy*, p. 7.

Robert Nelson writes about the BLM's grazing program costing $200 million annually while bringing in only $20 million in revenues in "How to Reform Grazing Policy: Creating Forage Rights on Federal Rangelands," *Fordham Environmental Law Journal*, 1997, 8(3): pp. 645–690.

The tongue-in-cheek reference to the western cattle rancher wanting "no interference from the government" is from James Michener, *Centennial*, Random House, New York, 1974.

Figures documenting the government's income from the Horse Butte grazing allotment and the yearly costs of the Interagency Bison Management Plan are from the United States Department of the Interior, National Park Service, *Bison Management Plan for the State of Montana and Yellowstone National Park, Final Environmental Impact Statement*, August 8, 2000, vol. I, pp. v, 195, 531–532, 534.

Jerry Jones's statement on private-property rights and the Endangered Species Act are from the Montana Stock Growers Association Web site, http://mtbeef.org/Who/leadership.htm (retrieved September 2001).

The suggestion of pressing charges against "landowners who refused our agents access to their lands" was made by Lon Mitchell in a letter to Dr. Clarence Siroky, Montana State Veterinarian, October 18, 1994.

The Department of Livestock's authority on private lands is spelled out in Montana Code Annotated, Section 81-2-101.

Representative Omar Conger's anti-bison views were recorded in the United States Congress, *The Congressional Globe*, 43rd Congress, 1st Session, Part 3, p. 2107.

Chapter Five ∞ Direct Action

Thoreau's quotation is from Henry David Thoreau, *Civil Disobedience, and Other Essays*, Dover, New York, 1993, p. 3.

Marsha Karle's quotation deflecting criticism of Yellowstone's involvement in the bison slaughter is from Scott McMillion, "Lethal Action: DOL Sends Bison to Slaughter Without Testing for Brucellosis," *Bozeman Daily Chronicle,* April 26, 2002.

The following three sources show that the Yellowstone bison population is still genetically intact: Natalie Herbert and James Derr, "A Comprehensive Evaluation of Cattle Introgression into US Federal Bison Herds," *Journal of Heredity*, vol. 98, 2007, pp. 1–12; Peter Dratch and Peter Gogan, *Bison Conservation Initiative: Bison Conservation Genetics Workshop: Report and Recommendations,* National Park Service, US Department of Interior, Natural Resource Program Center, Natural Resource Report NPS/NRPC/BRMD/ NRR-2010/257, National Park Service, Fort Collins, Colo.; and Mark Derr and R. Gehman. "Genetically, Bison Don't Measure Up to Frontier Ancestors," *The New York Times,* April 23, 2002, p. B23.

The scientist warning that the buffalo slaughter may be bringing about an "irreversible crippling of the gene pool" is Joe Templeton, "Testimony Before the Greater Yellowstone Interagency Brucellosis Committee," May 21, 1998.

Patrick Collins of APHIS is quoted in Joe Kolman, "Feds Pull Out of Bison Talks," *Billings Gazette*, December 16, 1999.

The study showing the significant difference between tissue and culture tests was conducted by Margaret Meyer and Mary Meagher, "Brucellosis in Free-Ranging Bison in Yellowstone, Grand Teton, and Wood Buffalo National Parks: A Review," *Journal of Wildlife Disease*, vol. 31, 1995, pp. 597–598.

Figures showing the results of culture tests versus blood tests on the 144 bison captured between 1997 and 1999 are from the United States Department of Agriculture: Animal and Plant Health Inspection Service, "Bison Serologies and Culture Results from 1997 to 1999," unpublished data, 2002.

Yellowstone Superintendent Mike Finley

Yellowstone Ranger Tom Mazzarisi warned of the dangers of giving the livestock industry control over wildlife in *Yellowstone Net Newsletter*, August 21, 1998.

The story of buffalo poacher Edgar Howell and how his capture led to passage of the Lacey Act of 1894 can be found in Paul Schullery, *Yellowstone's Ski Pioneers*, High Plains Publishing, Worland, Wyo., 1995, pp. 98–115, and Mary Meagher, *The Bison of Yellowstone National Park*, National Park Service, 1973, pp. 12, 17.

CPSIA
Printed
BVOW

3365

Atlanta-Fulton Public Library